GBU & GBA

ESCAPE
FROM THE BOX

Edward L. Hubbard

Edited by Art Nicolet

ESCAPE FROM THE BOX:
The Wonder of Human Potential

Praxis International, Inc.
West Chester, Pennsylvania

Published by arrangement with:
  Praxis International, Inc. by
  Positive Vectors, Inc.

For additional information or copies please contact:
  Positive Vectors, Inc.
  423 Pelham Road
  Fort Walton Beach, FL 32547
  ehubbard@gnt.net
  www.edhubbardpow.com

You may contact Praxis International, Inc. at 800-772-9472

Printed in the United States of America

Twelfth Printing: December 2009

Library of Congress Catalog Card Number: 93-87490

ISBN 0-9639231-0-2

BOOK DESIGN BY GREGORY V. GORE

To my Mother and Father, who gave me life, taught me values, supported my every decision, and never uttered even a whisper of complaint about the horrible burden I placed on their shoulders for six years, seven months and twelve days.

To the men and women who have worn the uniform and served in every corner of the Earth to protect and defend our great nation. To those who served and returned unmarked. To those who served and returned scarred for life. To those who were captured and lived to return. To those who served and gave their last full measure. To those who served and whose fate remains unknown–and to their families who still wait.

Acknowledgments

Rarely, if ever, is a book the result of the singular effort of one individual. Certainly this book is no exception. I would like to acknowledge the contribution of the many who made my dream become a reality:

The men and women with whom I worked in the U. S. Air Force who were the first to give my philosophy some credibility.

Bert and Bill Wycoff who launched my speaking career by asking the simple question, "Have you ever considered taking your show on the road?"

Nancy Putnam Greenawalt, my art teacher, who taught me to translate my thoughts onto canvas where everyone could see them.

Tom Nielsen, graphic artist for the Veterans Administration, who provided me a starting point for my painting, "Keep Faith."

Art Nicolet who asked for nothing in return except to be allowed to help guarantee this book would someday be published.

Bob Reid who, in one brief meeting, saw enough merit in my story to pass me onto Susanne and Greg Gore.

Susanne and Greg who believed they saw something of value in my rather crude and raw manuscript that was worth publishing and who performed the final editing on the manuscript.

And Jennifer, my wife, who has tolerated so much and allowed me to dream the impossible dream.

Contents

Prologue

Over the years that I have contemplated writing a book, I have, with some regularity, changed what I thought should be the title. I wanted a title that not only would catch the eye of a potential reader, but also one that would very concisely portray the content of that book. Each new title was the direct result of some significant event in my life that I call my "thought for the moment." However, even with all the title changes, the anticipated contents of this future book have changed little. Only the strength of my conviction and the breadth of my experience base have changed.

What started in 1983 to be nothing more than a satirical swipe at the Air Force to disprove some long-held myths, evolved into a serious attempt to correct or eliminate some of the frustration brought on by the bureaucracy. As I discovered that some of the things I talked about were actually being applied with dramatic results, my purpose *and* the right title for the book became clear. The events which crystallized my thinking follow.

In June 1983, I was notified that I had been selected for promotion to the rank of colonel in the U.S. Air Force, a rank technically referred to by the letter "O," a dash, and the number six (O-6, pronounced "oh six"). The letter "O" indicating officer and the number six meaning the sixth rank, starting with 0-1, 2nd Lieutenant.

First, the promotion confirmed my long standing belief that the Air Force bureaucracy makes so many mistakes each day, that if you stick around long enough, eventually they will err in your favor! My second thought was to capture the mood of that moment and express it in a book that would be basically satirical and hopefully humorous, while at the same time pointing out the unlimited potential of each individual regardless of the path chosen, or allowed to follow.

I had graduated very near the bottom of my high school class, enlisted in the Air Force Reserve during the summer prior to my senior year, and spent seven years as an enlisted man. I rarely got promoted because I always opted to go fly rather than take promotion tests. I applied for flying school (with no college) and was told by everyone I wasn't qualified. But, eventually I went! I graduated in July 1962. After receiving my navigator wings and commission, my commander told me that if I did well I would make major. If not, I would probably be thrown out as a captain. Over the next 20 years I would: (1) apply for and be rejected seven times for pilot training; (2) live the life of a second class citizen (navigator); (3) never be allowed to command even the tiniest Air Force organization; (4) offend virtually everyone with whom I worked because of my "natural ability" to express *exactly* what I thought; and, (5) be selected for promotion to the rank of colonel. Borrowing a phrase from the game of craps ("six, the hard way"), I chose for the title of my book, "0-6, The Hard Way." A book on how you do everything wrong (by some folks' standards) and still get promoted each time eligible.

The book never moved beyond the outline stage, but it evolved in the back of my mind. I was constantly adding new anecdotes, some for their humor but most for their "lessons learned" value. Then came an event that changed the title.

While in the Air Force, I contracted out some of my organization's work to the tune of approximately one million dollars of the taxpayers' hard earned money. It struck me that there must be a better solution, using resources already available.

I had a rather informal method of evaluating my employees' performance—one that would never meet the Government's (or probably anyone else's) standards. However, I never used my method for anything except to provide me with a gut feel for where we could make the greatest improvements. I assumed that every employee should be putting out a 100 percent effort during normal business hours. Then I would arbitrarily estimate each individual's level of effort. For example, if ten workers work at the following levels of effort: one at 120 percent; two at 100 percent; one at 80 percent; two at 70 percent; two at 50 percent; one at 30 percent; and one at 0 percent, their total effort is 670 percent. However, if all ten were putting out 100 percent, their total effort would be 1,000 percent. The difference, 330 percent, equates to 3.3 employees of lost effort. If there is more work to be done, 3.3 man years are being wasted. If all the work is being completed, there are 3.3 too many employees.

In my case, all required and desired work was being completed so I felt I had 3.3 extra people. Since it was never my intent to put people out of work, but to put people back to work, I needed something for these people to do. With just a little effort I determined that by using the extra people and hiring one new person (with unique qualifications not currently in our organization), I could terminate my outside contract and do the work in-house. By so doing we would significantly increase our in-house capacity. Additionally, we would greatly increase our flexibility and our ability to respond to no-notice requirement changes, a particularly critical issue. This new direction would also open the door to much more challenging and rewarding work for my employees and provide them greater career potential. All of those benefits, in and of themselves, made this an intelligent management decision. One other small side benefit should not be overlooked—a one million dollar per year cost reduction in our business expenses.

With all this in mind, I very confidently went off to brief my concept to my brigadier general boss. At the conclusion of my concept briefing, the general asked only one question: "Hubbard, why must you always row upstream?" He continued, "At a time when everyone else is attempting to contract Department of Defense work out to the private sector, why would you bring me a proposal to bring work back in house? Must you always go against the flow?" I merely reiterated the benefits and underlined the million dollar per year savings. As I was summarily dismissed, with not only a "no," but a "hell no" answer to my request, I could not resist answering the general's previous rhetorical question about rowing upstream. I said, "The reason I always row upstream is because I don't like where the rest of you are going—over the waterfall. If you are ever going to make any progress in today's world you must row upstream!" As everyone has surmised, my title was now "Rowing Upstream." The flavor of the book was taking on new dimension.

It was at about this same time that I became involved in motivational speaking. I simply started by explaining the valuable lessons we learned at the University of Adversity (the prisoner of war camps in North Vietnam) in an attempt to inspire others to greater effort. Within a couple of years I had amassed a reasonably lengthy list of accomplishments by those who accepted my theory and tried it.

One day, following a speech in which I had enumerated many of the accomplishments, I was asked, "Do you take credit for all those things other people accomplished?" I answered, "No, I didn't do any of the work. I merely sowed the seeds that allowed them to go try." Hence, the title of the "as yet to be written" book changed one more time: "I Sow the Seeds."

On the first day of August 1990, the major crystallizing event which I referred to earlier occurred. After more than

35 years of wearing the Air Force uniform, I retired. It was only a short time later that the correct title for my book came to light. Following a speaking engagement one night, a man, who had no military experience, asked me to characterize my 35 years in the Air Force. No one had ever asked me that question before. Essentially I explained to him my career was 35 years of being confined in a very tiny box, the dimensions of which were defined by the Air Force bureaucracy, and determined by them to be the "limits" of my capabilities. Notice that I refer to the Air Force *bureaucracy*, not to the uniform which I so proudly wore nor to the country which I so proudly served while wearing that uniform. Perhaps the greatest, possibly the only, satisfaction I received in the waning years of my career was the knowledge that every morning when my commander would check in my "box," I was always gone! I was out doing something someone else had determined to be beyond my capability. I had escaped from the box! Needless to say, there were a number of other Air Force officers who dedicated (read as wasted) a great deal of their time and energy attempting to return me to my box.

For one to understand the significance of my Houdini-like endeavor, one must review a small amount of my personal history. In April 1963, following two years in Undergraduate Navigator Training in Texas and Navigator Bombardier Training in California, I found myself en route to the Air Force Survival School at Stead Air Force Base, Nevada. I knew little about the school except that it lasted three weeks.

The first week was essentially classroom work. The second week started in the classroom, followed on Wednesday night by a three to four-hour crawl through a freezing snow-covered obstacle course that ended with "capture" and three days in a simulated POW camp. As part of the escape and evasion exercise, after "release" and one day of rest, we would then be off to the mountains for an 82 mile stroll on homemade snowshoes. (I lost 17 pounds in five days).

There was one other very subtle thing about survival school. It sort of fit into the "Oh, by the way" category. It was the "Black Box." Based on the previous experiences of men held captive in Communist countries, the "Black Box" became an integral part of simulated captivity. If one was to be successful in completing survival school, one must endure a session in the Black Box. Once placed in the Black Box, you could either wait until released or you could call the guard and declare an "academic situation." That meant the game was over and you wanted out RIGHT NOW. The significance of a failure to endure cannot be overstated. Students who flunked the survival school course go before a Flying Evaluation Board, lose their hard-earned wings–and are permanently grounded! So it was with considerable trepidation that one faced the Black Box.

I cannot tell you precisely when it was my turn in the Black Box. The first 36 hours in the simulated POW camp were spent in solitary confinement. Anytime I was removed from my four-foot cubical I had a bag over my head, so I never knew if it was day or night. When my time came for the box, it made no difference. I never actually saw the box, I only felt it. My first reaction as several people attempted to insert me into the box was, "I won't fit!" Needless to say, I did!

Life in the box was like nothing I had ever experienced. How long did it last? One hour—maybe two—perhaps only 30 minutes. I will never know, but I will always remember it was too long. When I was inserted, two or three people picked me up, put my feet in first, then squeezed me into a crouching position and pushed. My arms were stuffed in wherever they could find space. Then they simply shoehorned me in until the box was full. Whatever position my anatomy was in when the door closed, was the position it would be in until the door reopened. I was squeezed in so tightly, breathing was even difficult. I could barely inhale. The only things I could move were my fingers. That allowed me to use the fingers of my right hand to work the bag off of my head. It was still pitch black, but at least I could breathe easier. With the fingers of my left hand I could scratch the back side of my right leg, just above the ankle. Unfortunately, that is not where I itched!

I endured. When I was removed from the box, every part of my body except my brain was asleep. I couldn't stand or walk for some time. Eventually, I returned to my spacious four-foot cubical. As I stretched out in the darkness I thought to myself with enormous pride, "I escaped from the box!" On that cold spring day in 1963, at the ripe old age of 24, I felt that I had just endured one of the most difficult challenges I would face in life. Little did I know.

Nearly ten years later to the day, in March 1973, I escaped from another box. I was released after having spent 2,420 days (six years, seven months and twelve days) as a prisoner of war in North Vietnam. That wonderful feeling of freedom I had basked in following my escape from the Black Box in 1963 truly became trivial when compared to the enormous feeling of freedom I enjoyed in 1973.

It would be 17 more years before I would achieve my ultimate Houdini feat: escape from the box of bureaucracy. I have never known such total freedom. I now own my own corporation and answer to no one–except my wife. I recognize and accept no limits. For the first time in my life I am truly free to do as much (or as little) as I decide. When asked, "Can you do four speeches in a 24-hour period?" I say, "Yes." "How about 8:00 a.m. Tuesday in Orlando, 1:00 p.m. Tuesday in Fort Worth, 7:00 p.m. Tuesday in Los Angeles, and 8:00 a.m. Wednesday in Salt Lake City?" The reply is still yes–if the airplanes all leave on time. The answer to your question is "yes." I did try to meet all four of those commitments and succeeded. The only tight spot occurred when I arrived in Salt Lake City 20 minutes prior to the start of the event. I walked in the door in the middle of my introduction! I had always been capable of doing that, but never allowed to try!

It seems we all spend our lives confined to our box. Frequently the dimensions are determined by someone else, or by society. Some of the best known dimensions are: skin color, sex, religion, (or lack thereof), age, SAT scores, or the best known of all–your IQ. Louis Tice once remarked, "IQ is one of the greatest injustices ever perpetrated on mankind." Unfortunately, all too often the dimensions of one's box are self-imposed.

This book, a long time in the writing and with its ever-changing title, has but one single purpose. I hope to provide the inspiration necessary so that each person can "escape from the box" and make his or her contribution.

PART ONE

Human Potential

FREEDOM

Not too very long after my encounter with the survival school "Black Box," I found myself making the wearisome trip from my last Air Force assignment in California to my new assignment in South Carolina. The arduousness of the journey, however, was tempered somewhat by the mere fact that under the hood of my 1959 Chevy Impala were more horses than would have made up an entire wagon train on the same trip 100 years earlier.

As we climbed the western slope of Berthoud Pass, I noted with enthusiasm that the road had been straightened and widened considerably, and a passing lane all the way to the top had been added. One of the most dangerous bottlenecks in Colorado had been removed since the last time I had passed that way. We no longer had to creep along at five miles per hour behind a long line of trucks, waiting our golden opportunity to risk our lives to move a few feet ahead in the parade. Looking back almost 30 years, I can still remember my thoughts as I lazily urged my "350 horses" toward 80 miles per hour.

I was awed by the thought of how easily I coasted over the top of the perilous Berthoud Pass at more than 11,000 feet above sea level, compared to the staggering effort necessary to make the same crossing in a covered wagon. For the first time in my life, I had a true appreciation of how difficult life could be, or had been, for others (possibly because of my recent visit to the Black Box). It certainly would not be the last time I thought about such subjects.

In the summer of 1990, one of my last official sojourns for the Air Force was to my detachment at Holloman Air Force Base in Alamagordo, New Mexico. I have made that trip many times. My favorite part of the trip is the one hour and thirty minute drive across the barren, desolate waste-land between El Paso and Alamagordo on U.S. Highway 54.

As it turns out, I have driven virtually every single mile of Highway 54, from its eastern terminus, just east of Mark Twain's boyhood home of Hannibal, Missouri, until it falls into the Rio Grande river in El Paso, Texas. All my life I have been kidded by people who drove west in my home state of Kansas, some on Highway 54. All they could talk about was the vast nothingness of western Kansas. None of those people, obviously, ever drove the stretch from Alamagordo to El Paso!

Each time I departed the suburbs of North El Paso I recalled my thoughts of many years earlier, when I casually traversed the western slopes of Berthoud Pass. For those of you who have never had the privilege, Highway 54 runs almost due north from El Paso. For the next 90 miles there is only one bend in the road. Parallelling the highway some 50 miles to the east is the Guadalupe Mountain range. To the west, but somewhat closer, is a more rugged range of mountains. During the 90-minute drive I was always con-sumed with my wonderment about the early American settlers who crossed this area. I tried to imagine what must have gone through their minds.

After days, or even weeks, of struggling to get their wagons over the mountains east of today's Highway 54, they were greeted with the reward that it was only about 80 to 100 miles across a barren, desolate wasteland before they had to attack the Organ Mountains which, at least, were smaller than the Rockies around Berthoud Pass.

The feelings I experienced in the spring of 1963 at Berthoud Pass and in the summer of 1990 in southeastern New Mexico were the same. They were feelings of amazement and bewilderment. What kind of people were those early Americans? What enabled them to persevere under such adverse circumstances? Why had they been able to accomplish what so few today would even be willing to consider?

I believe they wanted to be free. They wanted to escape from the box and they were committed to making that happen. Is it possible that the Americans of today lack that level of commitment, or could it be that we have just become so irresponsible and greedy that we no longer care? I have had a couple of interesting conversations with non-Americans concerning our lack of commitment.

While hanging around Ho Chi Minh's jail house in the fall of 1967, I had the unfortunate opportunity to become part of a small, randomly selected group of ten American POWs who fell under the purview of two Cuban interrogators for one full year. It was one of the most difficult periods of our incarceration, but it did have its lighter moments. In the summer of 1968, the door frame to our cell rotted off and the frame just collapsed onto the porch. The head of the Cuban team, a big and exceptionally nasty individual, whom we called Fidel, decided we would fix the door. He provided us with an odd assortment of boards, a few nails, a couple of large stove bolts and a miniature sledge hammer.

We quickly determined that the boards were too short to make the door frame, so we decided to notch two lengths of four-by-fours and splice them together. We requested a drill from Fidel to make holes for the stove bolts. Fidel responded that we didn't need a drill. I will never forget his words, "You know the problem with you Americans, you don't have enough commitment. With enough commitment an elephant can f - - - an ant!" And with that said, Fidel proceeded to take two stove bolts, about as big around as a thumb and blunt on the end, and drive them like nails through the four-by-fours. Though not exactly a classical philosopher, Fidel did provide us with some food for thought.

More recently, following a speech I had given in San Jose, California, I was invited to join about a dozen members of the audience for dinner. Luck of the draw put me next to a very gracious and articulate Japanese lady. She told me she had spent the first 20 years of her life in Japan and the second 20 in the United States, but she frequently traveled back to Japan. During dinner we discussed, at great length, the enormous success Japan had achieved since the end of World War II. Her explanation was rather simple. She said, "You Americans think the Japanese are the cleverest people on Earth. You are wrong. Americans are the cleverest people on Earth. You invent everything, we copy it—better! You never follow through. You have no commitment to anything, with the exception, perhaps, of a quick dollar."

Were both of these outsiders, though clearly from different backgrounds, able to read something in our culture that we have either overlooked, or perhaps refused to see? Lack of commitment certainly appears to be one of our shortcomings, but, I suspect it is only one of a long list of hurdles we must clear. Before we can make that all important commitment, I believe it is essential that we recognize the need to escape from the box, and then believe that escape is possible. And of course, there will always be the ever-present question, "What is in this for me?"

I can answer that question with one word: FREEDOM! What caused people to leave everything behind them and immigrate to this country? The same promise that led some of the same people to also endure the incredible hardships of Berthoud Pass and southeastern New Mexico: FREE-DOM.

We must change our view of the world, our perceptions and our attitudes, or we will be destined to live in the box with limitations as defined by others. Our forefathers were unwilling to accept that fate. How about you?

Do you have the courage to try? I can show you how to escape from the box. Only you can make the decision to try, and that decision will be driven by your attitude!

Let me share my attitude and my view of the world. After the President of the United States designated July 20, 1984 to be National Prisoner of War and Missing in Action Day, the Veterans Administration published a poster similar to the left half side of the picture on the cover of this book. When I saw the poster, I felt that it truly reflected all the frustration and futility of captivity. It showed the eagle with the chain on his leg, the barbed wire fence and guard tower. As I looked at the painting, however, the image bothered me considerably because I believe the positive side of life is much more important than the negative side. I am so convinced of that fact that I spend most of my time traveling across the country speaking about the positive side of life. However, I felt that the painting could have a great message if the positive side of life could be included.

I made about a thousand calls and I eventually cornered the man who painted that original eagle. He is Tom Nielsen, a graphic artist with the Veterans Administration in Washington. I told him, "Tom, I think that is a very intelligent picture, but you never finished it. It would have been nice if you had done the positive side of life also." He told me that he had never even thought about that, so I requested and received his permission to take his concept and expand it to include the positive.

What you see on the front cover of this book is the result, a reproduction of an oil painting I did in 1984. Essentially, Tom saw the eagle as representing those in captivity. I saw the eagle a lot bigger than Tom did. That's our national emblem. In my painting, the eagle represents every American. It could be you, it could be anybody else. The chain on the eagle's foot represents all the burdens you have, or perceive that you have, which you are dragging around in the world, i.e., your ball and chain! It could be anything—it could be folks who smoke and wish they could quit. It could be folks who drink and wish they could quit. It could be folks who are married and wish they could quit! It could be folks who have jobs they would like to quit. It could be folks with jobs they perceive to be too difficult to do with the resources they have been given. Whatever your perceptions are, whatever you see as your burdens in this life, that's what that chain is meant to represent. The left-hand part of my painting represents the difficult part of life. Unfortunately, it will always be there.

The right-hand part of my painting represents the hope for the future. I added the Statue of Liberty. I think you all know what that represents. It represents freedom! In my mind, and in my painting, it represents freedom from everything including all of your burdens and all the perceived limitations which prevent you from reaching for your full potential.

The most important part of my picture is the little ray of sunshine that comes down behind the cloud and shines on the Statue of Liberty. This represents the little ray of sunshine that comes down into your life every day if you just know where to look for it. It is the idea that something good happens in your life every day, which is how I see the world. The title of my painting is *KEEP FAITH*. If you can believe in the meaning of the painting, if you can learn to accept my view of the world and you keep faith, it is possible you won't ever have any bad days again for the rest of your life!

ALL GOOD DAYS

Let me establish a common reference point for the rest of this book by telling you about one long day in my life. See if you think it was a good day or a bad day. It's important that you know what I think a bad day is and that we all agree on what a bad day is. Back on the 20th of July 1966, I got up at 2:00 a.m. to go to work. I discovered many years ago that if you get up at two o'clock in the morning to go to work, chances are you are going to have a bad day. It tends to work out that way. On that particular day I took a short stroll to the officer's club at Tahkli Air Base in Thailand where I was stationed. In Thailand, if you haven't ever been there, the menus were under plastic and the waiters used a grease pencil to draw a line through things as they ran out. On this particular morning they were out of everything except donuts. So, everybody said let's have donuts for breakfast. You could get two donuts for ten cents. I cut into the first donut and my plate filled up with grease. That was the second indication of how my day was going to go. I did not like the trend so far. I did something I regretted for a long time–I went off to work that morning on an empty stomach. I left those greasy donuts on the table.

I arrived at my squadron at 4:30 a.m. and was briefed on a flight to North Vietnam. At 6:30 a.m. I went out to the flight line, climbed into my jet, took off and flew up to North Vietnam. I milled around the sky for about an hour and thirty minutes, and somewhere around 8:00 a.m. I very cleverly intercepted a couple of surface-to-air missiles with my airplane. Do you know what happens when you do that? The missiles make a million little holes in your airplane. The aircraft maintenance crew is not impressed when the airplane comes back full of holes. That particular day the maintenance crew wasn't any problem because we had so many holes in the airplane that three minutes later we were going straight down somewhere around 600 miles per hour. I no longer had any wings on my airplane. Being a reasonably prudent guy, I jumped out. Have you ever jumped out of an airplane? Ever jumped out at 600 miles an hour? Allow me to explain how fast 600 miles an hour really is. At 600 miles per hour you are traveling roughly the equivalent of three football fields per second. Let me tell you what this speed does. It really waters your eyes. Seriously. It takes your eyebrows and puts them right back on the back of your head. It's a real attention getter and it's something you don't forget right away.

After my parachute blossomed, I opened my eyes to find that I was blind. That was possibly the most frightening moment in my life. When I reached up and checked my face, I discovered I wasn't really blind. The airplane was going so fast when I ejected, that my helmet spun around backwards. I was looking into the back of my helmet. But I was very successful. I ejected far beyond the red-line speed recommended for safe ejection from that particular aircraft and successfully made it to the ground with minor scrapes and bruises. I wandered around in the jungle for about eight and a half hours playing hide-and-go-seek with the North Vietnamese. Between 4:00 and 5:00 p.m., I was captured. That day I began the first of what turned out to be 2,420 days, a little over six and a half years, as a prisoner of war. Would you say that's a bad day? Think that qualifies? One of the first realizations I had in prison was that every life event is good or bad relative to something else. In reviewing my life events of the first 28 years, I decided that July 20, 1966 was a relatively bad day.

A more recent event which took place in January 1987 will give you a much better feel for what I see as a bad day. I went to Charleston AFB in South Carolina to speak at the commencement of an Air Force leadership school. I arrived on Wednesday afternoon to speak on Thursday night and was met by an incredibly ambitious technical sergeant who was my host and escort. He picked me up at the airport and we drove across to the other side of the base to the billeting office. En route he said, "You know, I was thinking that you weren't scheduled to speak until tomorrow night. I didn't want you to be bored all day tomorrow, so I've scheduled you to speak four times." I said, "Thank you very much, I was hoping you would do that!" I had never tried to speak four times in one day. I had no idea if I could even do that. However I thought, "Since I'm signed up, I guess I will at least try it. You never know until you try!"

I went to bed fairly early that night to get a little extra rest, woke up at 5:00 a.m. the next morning and never felt better in my life. I thought, "I could conquer the world today if I really got serious." I felt so good I decided I had better knock the edge off that great feeling, so I got up and exercised for a while. Then I took my shower and shaved, went to the closet and took out the uniform which I always wore when speaking to Air Force personnel. I took my coat off the hanger and discovered I had forgotten to bring my pants! Do you want to know what a bad day is? It's when you get up in the morning, have to stand in front of your audience and you have no pants to wear! That's what a bad day really looks like.

When you wake up in the morning and things don't go the way you planned them, or things start falling apart early on (like you forget your pants or worse, your plane gets shot down), or later in the day, when things don't go as advertised, *the attitude that you take at that point in time is going to be critical to the outcome of the day, and determines whether the day is going to be a success or a failure, whether you are going to have a good day or a bad day.*

I was born with a bad attitude. Along the way it didn't get any better. The day I was shot down you can safely assume I had a bad attitude. I had gotten up at 2:00 a.m., and given the choice of greasy donuts, left for work on an empty stomach. By the time I was captured that afternoon, I had the worst attitude of anybody you have ever met. When I went to prison I had run out of resources. What I had left in my world that day and for the following six and a half years were one very large handful of bad attitude and one very large handful of self-pity. If I had retained that bad attitude and self-pity and looked for nothing more, I think you can assume I would have had 2,420 bad days.

In December 1966, 150 days after my capture, by a twist of fate I found myself in solitary confinement in a tiny room, six feet square. I had been there for 28 days. It took me three steps to walk diagonally across the room. About three days before Christmas I was pacing the floor talking to myself, trying to figure out what I was going to do on Christmas Day, my first big holiday as a prisoner of war. I wasn't quite sure how I was supposed to entertain myself. I assumed I would have a psychological problem. I didn't know how big it would be, or how I was going to deal with it. As I paced the floor trying to come up with a plan, I remembered a story I had heard as a little boy. It was about a man who felt sorry for himself because he had no shoes, until he met a man who had no feet. I don't know if you have ever heard that story. Just in case you don't understand the meaning of it, let me explain. No matter how bad your day looks, no matter how tough the situation is, if you take a look around, there's always somebody who has it a little tougher than you do. That particular day, locked up in a tiny little cell, ten thousand miles from home, all by myself, I sat down on the concrete floor and I thought about that story! I convinced myself that probably more than 99 percent of the people in the world had it worse than I did that day.

For starters, I was an American. That's as good as it ever gets. I don't care where you are or what you are doing, that's as good as it's ever going to get. Along with that, I was only temporarily locked up. Though I couldn't foresee the future, someday I would come home and I would travel and do speeches with all expenses paid and write a book! Basically I didn't have a bad deal. I just had to be a little more patient. That day my view of the world changed dramatically. Probably, that is the day my painting *Keep*

Faith started to form in the back of my brain. Even more importantly, my attitude changed that day. For the first time ever, I was able to make some critical decisions about the future of my life.

The first thing I decided was, by God, I am going to survive. For the first 150 days, I sincerely did not believe that. I was absolutely convinced I would die in that prison. I just didn't know when or how, but I was sure that was my fate. Dying was not mandatory. That had only been my perception. If I could change my perception, perhaps I could change the outcome. And I did. I'm not quite sure why, but certainly my change in perception had something to do with my change in attitude. One of the other realizations I made that day was that I ought to be smart enough to be able to turn this into a productive experience. I wasn't quite sure how to do it but what I didn't know that day was that I had six more years to practice. Not a bad deal!

I also discovered how miserable life could really be sitting around feeling sorry for myself. I promised myself then that I would never do that again. I didn't care what happened after that, no matter how bad it got, I promised myself I would never fall back into the trap of sitting around wallowing in self-pity. That's a horrible way to live! The most important decision I made that day was that never, ever again would I allow myself to have a bad day. Last Christmas was 26 years since I made that commitment. In those 26 years, I have never had a bad day. I've had a couple that weren't so great–the day I forgot my pants wasn't so great, but over the long haul it's been very good. You must never forget, it's all relative.

OPPORTUNITIES TO EXCEL

While in that prison we had nothing to do. There was nothing in our cells except us, so we spent a lot of time thinking. We thought about everything you have ever thought about in your whole life. We thought about thousands of things you have not thought about yet. But over those years and the millions of ideas and concepts we discussed and thought about, there was one idea that we never talked about. No one ever suggested it and it never came up in conversation. That was the idea of doing exactly what I have been doing for the last several years, getting groups of people together and talking about life in a North Vietnamese prison camp. If you look back with me, I think it will be rather obvious to you why we felt that our experiences would not be worth talking about. We realized while we were in prison that there were literally thousands of events occurring every day that were important, up to and including man going to the moon for the first time. But not one of them was happening where we were. At least, that was our perception. So we assumed that when we came back we would have very, very little of interest to talk about.

Two or three days after my release in 1973, I made some very amazing discoveries in connection with reentering society. One of the first was that all that I had taken to prison with me, the things that truly became valuable, simple things like faith, pride, courage, hope and lots of intangibles–intangibles you think about and talk about all of your life but never ever fully understand–were what this country lost during the Vietnam War. During the time we were in captivity in North Vietnam, this country lost its sense of direction. This country lost confidence in its ability to do anything right. I have been back for more than 20 years and over those 20 plus years we have come an amazing way toward recovering. We still have a long, long way to go and I am counting on every one of you to become a player in bringing this country back to its basic values.

When we came home and saw how screwed up the country had become in our absence, we realized how fortunate we were to have been on the other side of the world in a totally different environment. We were fortunate to have been involved in a larger effort that allowed us to retain those intangibles that many people had lost. That's when we discovered how important our experience had been. The experience we had is not valuable only to those of us who sat in prison. That experience is valuable to everyone in this country. If we can ever explain to you in some small way what we learned there, and how to use that knowledge to improve your life a little each day, and how to apply it to all the challenges we are trying to meet in this country and all the problems we are trying to solve, then our captivity was not a waste of our time. It was the greatest education we will ever get and sharing the experiences can benefit the entire nation. The primary reason I travel around the country to speak and the reason for this book is that I believe we have learned some lessons that can only be learned in a prison-like environment. Hopefully, as I share these lessons you can learn from them too.

I am not going to bore you with lots of gory details and war stories of what happened in prison. I could fill a book with horror stories which some of you would not even be able to comprehend and would serve no purpose nor provide value. Instead, I want to take a different approach to describing our experiences by explaining the positive aspects of being a prisoner of war, something I believe you will find valuable. If you have read the paper lately and looked at all the news, between the budget cuts, corporate downsizing, health care reform, and many other current subjects, I think you are probably all aware of a perception today in this country, and probably a little wider spread than just this country, that we all face the same challenge—how to do more with less. Have you ever talked about that? That's all we talked about in the Air Force.

In an era of diminishing resources, doing more with less has become a reality and a requirement. As you attempt to deal with this reality, you will encounter a group I call the "doom and gloom" guys. You have all met them. They are the people who are always standing there when you are trying to make improvements. They will give you 15 to 20 reasons why it can't be done. These people were put on this earth to make sure we don't ever make any progress. I was put here to guarantee they fail. I was put here to convince you that we *can* do more with less.

I have two life experiences I feel that uniquely qualify me to address the subject of doing more with less from a personal perspective. First, sitting around in prison for six and a half years gave me a great opportunity to examine every event in my life. In each case where a decision was required between option A and option B, I found, under closer scrutiny, that there were hundreds of other options I had overlooked. I greatly expanded my horizons as I viewed new opportunities. The other experience was 35 years of wearing the Air Force uniform.

One of the great advantages of being in the military is that any time somebody places a hurdle out there that is a little tough to climb over, we all rally around and somebody thinks up a clever little cliché. We all grab onto it and run out and conquer whatever it is we are after. We learned to be very creative. Several years ago, I attended a meeting which the leader started by showing a slide entitled, "Problems to Solve Today." The slide listed about 20 items. As always, in any crowd, there is at least one person with a better idea. As it turned out, in this case, the individual really did have a better idea. In fact, it was one of the best I have ever heard. He suggested we change the title of the slide from "Problems to Solve Today," to "Opportunities to Excel Today." With that simple change we moved from a negative mood to a positive mood. What had originally appeared to be a formidable task suddenly appeared doable, and later proved to be relatively simple. Not only that, we left the meeting with a new concept of operations called "opportunity to excel." I was going to carry that new cliché with me for the rest of my life.

Do you want to know what "Opportunity to Excel" really means? It means that if I'm your boss, I just thought of one more task for you to accomplish in addition to everything else you are doing. When I need something done I just walk down the hall and point at the first person who sticks their head out the door and say, "I have an opportunity for you to excel," which means you are going to have to work a little harder than you did before. Please think about that saying within a slightly larger context. Each one of us has many opportunities to excel every day of our lives. This is the opportunity to do something personally or professionally that you have never done before. These opportunities will come by all day, every day you are alive. With each opportunity to excel will be a concurrent opportunity that does not excite Americans. A decision must be made. How am I going to accomplish this? The first thing most Americans do is to hold out their hands and say give me some more resources, frequently measured in dollars, and I'll show you how easy it is to do.

I want to convince you that expecting to receive additional resources every time you hold out your hand is not the correct answer. It never has been and never will be. It is in fact counterproductive to what you need to accomplish in your life. What you really want to accomplish is a greater effort–neither measured by working longer hours nor measured in carrying a heavier load–but measured by performing better and smarter than ever before. Simpler if possible. Today, that performance level is becoming mandatory. Now is the time for a new approach. Now is the time to stop talking about whether we can do things. Now is the time to start talking about "How soon can we start and how soon can we finish?" and "How can we do the job with the resources already available?" That's the direction we must take. I truly believe our reluctance to go out and attempt this greater effort stems from a lack of confidence, if you will, in our ability to achieve anything greater than that which we are already achieving. Stop and think about it, when you have an opportunity to excel, the first thought that goes through your mind is, "I'm already maxed out. I'm doing more than I get paid for, and I'm doing more than anybody else in this company." We all feel that way every day.

When we flew combat in North Vietnam, that's precisely how we felt. We were up milling around in the sky. The guys on the ground were shooting at us with real bullets—relatively high risk. We all assumed it would be the most difficult task we would ever perform and we assumed we were operating at our limit. We placed a mark at the very top of our wall indicating that limit. Seconds after we hit the ground in North Vietnam we found out we were wrong. Our life events to that point suddenly became insignificant compared to the challenge that started the next day. Quite by accident, we were thrown into an environment where we had to exceed any previous effort in our lives, physically and mentally every day, just to stay alive. We finally discovered just how much more was available to each of us every day. If we had refused to go beyond the limit mark we had placed on the wall, we would have all died in captivity for lack of an adequate effort. We found out how much more was available.

INCREMENTAL IMPROVEMENT

I want to make a broad assumption. I'm going to assume you have achieved a significant number of accomplishments in your life already. It is not my intent to belittle those accomplishments. My intent is to convince you that no matter what you have done, no matter how great it is, no matter how many rewards you have received, not you, not me, not one of us on the face of the earth will ever achieve our full potential as a human being. We haven't even scratched the surface yet. What I want to do is to open the door just a crack, allow you a peek at the strange world where we lived for a few years, and give you a view of what might be in your future if you want it. I want to send you on your way to see what you can accomplish.

Until the day we were shot down and captured, we saw the world precisely the same way as everyone else. Then suddenly, we were thrown into a world where there were not many good deals. However, there were a few good deals and that is what I will concentrate on. Interestingly enough, mixed in among the few good deals we even had one luxury. Perhaps you didn't realize we had a luxury in prison. It was a luxury you will probably never enjoy in America. Certainly it is something you have heard about all of your life, something you have always wanted, but probably will never have. It's a thing called spare time. I want you to think about this. If I were to lock you in your bathroom or closet for the next six and one half years, how much spare time do you think you would have? I bet it would be a bunch!

Allow me to explain why I consider spare time a luxury. Simply, it allows you to do something unique. It allows you to go back and review your entire life in as much detail as you would like and as many times as you would like. I consider that opportunity to be one of the most valuable experiences of my life.

When I was shot down I was 28 years old. For all practical purposes I had my whole life of 28 years that I could review from A to Z. I did that quite a few times. I reviewed each event that I could remember. I did that hundreds of times. When I arrived at the end of my review, I always came to exactly the same conclusion: every single thing that I had ever done in my entire life, for 28 years, I could have done better with just a tiny bit more effort. That is still true, but at least now I understand and am working on it. It is also true for everyone of you.

Try to imagine, if you can, how discouraging and disheartening it is to wake up one day at the age of 28 and suddenly realize that everything you have done in your entire life could have been done better. When you couple that realization with the fact that this discovery was made while sitting in a prison on the other side of the world, the impact is devastating to your morale. Then fortunes turned. I was allowed to live with another prisoner. A review of his life indicated he was doing no better. I felt better. Together, we then took the liberty of reviewing the lives of many of our friends and relatives, people we had known and worked with for many years. We discovered no one was doing any better than we were. We both felt better.

It became our belief that Americans, as a society, go through life operating at a level of effort considered to be quite significant. When we compared the new standards we were required to live by in captivity, the ordinary American effort became insignificant. We found out how much more was available to each of us. It was this realization that perhaps led to one of the most important changes of my view of the world in general and my management style in particular. My world would never look the same again.

When I returned home, each time I received a new assignment, I would call a meeting of all the folks who were going to be directly under my control. After introducing myself, I would simply explain the goal I held for each individual:

"I expect each of you to do everything you do today slightly better than yesterday. The goal tomorrow will be to do everything better than you did today and I expect that to continue from this day forward. Incremental and continuous improvement. I will not tell you how to do your job because I am quite confident you know more about your job than I do. Besides, if I have to tell you what to do, I don't need your help. I want this to be your new thought process, your new way of life. We are going to improve everything we do every day."

Can you visualize the reaction those comments elicited from a room full of total strangers? Here's this new guy in town and without so much as a "Howdy, how are you?" and no clue as to what the organization does for a living, or how well personnel perform their tasks, he announces the obvious need for improvement. The response was generally negative, as I expected it to be. In several organizations, during the early years of this concept, there was widespread nonacceptance of my belief. It was obvious I desperately needed a method to prove my point. I needed a method so convincing that no one could challenge my assumptions. I needed a method whereby they would merely accept my assumptions and march off to try them.

By a twist of fate, the 3M Corporation came to my rescue. They introduced a new product at this precise time which filled my need perfectly. The new product was called a *Post-it,* a small yellow piece of paper with some sticky stuff on the back. The *Post-it* was advertised to have a thousand uses. Well, I discovered use number one thousand and one! I selected the size next to the smallest, about one and a half inches square, and adopted it as my lifetime training aid. I tell each audience that a single *Post-it* will be a lifetime supply of all the understanding they will need to understand and accept my concept of continuous improvement! During my presentations, I have provided perhaps a quarter of a million of these tiny, virtually free and yet priceless reminders. Along with the *Post-it,* I also provide simple directions for use:

Take your personal *Post-it* and stick it on your bathroom mirror, where you will see it every morning of your life. On that tiny piece of paper, list everything you have ever done in your entire life, personally and professionally, that you did so well it can never be improved upon. See if that provides any new perspective to your life.

To the best of my knowledge, no one has ever written anything on their *Post-it.* I must admit that one lady did suggest she felt she would be hard-pressed to improve upon how she brought her daughter into the world. I am prepared to concede that solitary act by any woman, but I also do not anticipate anyone running out of space on their *Post-it* anytime soon.

So that you do not have to wait for me to happen through your part of the world, here is your very own *Post-it*. It's my investment in your future!

ATTITUDE

As I sat in prison, discovering my life wasn't going too well, I realized I had better take action. I sat down and decided to make a serious plan to fix my life. Not so that I would be perfect–you cannot get there from here–but just to improve a little bit every day! I worked on that plan over the next five years. As I did, I evolved my own personal philosophy of life. I think you can benefit from my philosophy. It is very simple. I believe that human potential is nothing more than a state of mind. Your state of mind, or potential, is controlled by two things: what you think you can do, and how hard you are willing to work to accomplish it. That's all! Absolutely nothing else plays in that equation. It doesn't make any difference what your boss would like for you to do, or your parents or anyone else. It has absolutely nothing to do with training or education. Those are only aids to get to what we want. It has nothing to do with IQ because I believe that we don't even know what IQ measures. It depends entirely on you and what you sincerely believe you can do and how hard you are willing to work. Don't ask me how I arrived at that conclusion. It just evolved over a long period of time.

When I was shot down I was 28 years old. Up until that day I had no direction in my life whatsoever. I had no focus whatsoever. I was drifting along having a good time. I thought that all there was in this world was having a good time. I was doing that very well. In the spring of 1971, after I had been in prison for almost five years, I had a very interesting experience early one morning. It was probably one of the most important events in my life. It suddenly put my life clearly in focus and it has been clearly in focus ever since. I awoke at 5:00 a.m. that morning and started jumping rope as I did every morning. I had been jumping rope for almost an hour nonstop and had not missed. I was just two or three minutes from setting a world record in jump rope.

As I jumped, a man who lived with me walked by and intentionally stuck his finger in the rope and caused me to miss. I was pretty rash in those days and my first instinct was to pick up the rope, wrap it around his neck and jerk his head off. Seemed like a pretty good plan until I took a look at how big he was. I decided that wasn't very prudent, so in a way that very few people could duplicate, and being as rude as anybody you have ever met, I walked over to this guy and I had a very short talk with him. We talked about his ancestors and we talked about how I didn't particularly care for some of his habits. Then I rudely walked away.

I was very lucky because I lived with another American who was only three years older than I was but probably a couple of hundred years smarter at least. He saw what I did and he called me over. He said, "Come here! Sit down. I saw how you treated that guy. I want to counsel you." Now, I don't know about you, but if you have my personality, counseling is rather routine. I have been counseled all my life so it was no big deal. This man had moved in with me about a year before and by noon the first day we were together, he stopped me as I was walking by in the cell, and he said, "You know what? Bar none, without any exceptions, you have the worst attitude of anybody I have ever met in my whole life. Given your small size, and your incredible attitude, I am amazed you're still alive!" He really thought I was in trouble. He decided he would adopt me. "My goal is to get you out of prison alive. If I'm smart enough to pull that off, my second goal would be to return you to the United States as a productive citizen. Given your attitude, I don't know if I will succeed, but I will try." He tried every day for the next year, unsuccessfully.

On the day of the jump rope incident, when I sat down next to him he said, "I know something that you don't know but something you desperately need to know." He continued with this admonishment, "What we are receiving in this prison is the most expensive education you are ever going to get in your entire life. We came dangerously close to dying to be enrolled here. In this school, each day for the last five years you have had an equal opportunity to die or to stay enrolled here. We have paid a very high price. Now is the time to reap the rewards. The day you leave here is going to be critical. You must leave the horrors of this experience behind, and you must take the valuable lessons we have learned home and use them to improve the rest of your life." This has to be the most intelligent thought I have ever heard in my life. He told me that more than 20 years ago, and I think about that every day. I think about what it meant then and what it still means to me today.

I want to provide you some insight to the valuable lessons my cell mate was talking about over 20 years ago. I want to share a little bit about how those lessons affected our lives in prison and a little bit about how they have affected our lives since we returned. Most importantly, I want to share how I think those lessons can affect your life and your state of mind. You see, if I can influence the way you think just a very, very small amount, I believe you will greatly change the way you act for the rest of your life. You *can* change your attitude about the world. The minute that happens, without a push from anybody, each of you will quietly steal away and attempt this greater effort that I mentioned earlier. In an instant, no matter what your pay grade or job title, no matter what your status in society used to be, you will immediately become a leader in your community. Everybody will rally around you because of your positive attitude. You are going to grow and benefit from that attitude. Everyone around you will benefit. The bottom line is that The United States of America will benefit, and that's why I go around the country to speak to people. That's why I wrote this book.

When you look at the world today, even with the positive changes in Europe, there is total chaos in virtually every part of the world. The entire world is searching and screaming for some leadership. There is nobody in the world who is better prepared and better qualified to provide that leadership than the citizens of this country! That is not something that you ought to take lightly! It is an awesome responsibility we have as citizens of this country. If we do not step up and assume the leadership role in this country and in the world, we may never get another chance in our lifetimes. It is critical. All I ask is that you consider becoming a participant.

COMPETITION

As a method for explaining the valuable lessons we learned, I will recount my favorite war stories. Most people like a war story and each one has a lesson to be learned and hopefully the lessons will be things you can take away with you and use. First let me ask you one question. Have you ever spent even 30 seconds of your life trying to determine the common thread that runs through our society that made this country so great? It is something you have been involved in all your life. It is critical to your survival. You possibly do not understand its value and importance because it has never been taken away from you. It is competition. Do you realize that we compete in virtually all we do every day? If it's a good deal, you try to get to the head of the line. Just watch what happens in church every Sunday. Everyone competes to sit in the back of church. You compete in everything you do. You do it for very good reasons. Competition gives your life direction, so you know which way to go when you get up each day. It forces you, at least subconsciously, to set goals so you can tell if you are making any progress in life. But, most importantly, competition is the force that makes your life productive. When life ceases to be productive what results is the most empty and worthless feeling on earth. You can never appreciate the value of competition until it is removed from your life. Drug addicts and alcoholics are among the folks who truly understand that feeling. Several years ago, following a speech in South Florida, a young man from the audience approached me. He said, "You are the first person

I ever met who truly understands how I feel. I was on drugs for five years. I have been clean for the last eighteen months. I honestly have a five-year total void in my life."

Fortunately, we didn't have to do drugs or alcohol to learn about an unproductive life. We went to prison! When you arrive in prison, the first thing that happens is that they take everything you own including your underwear. They tie you up and throw your naked body on the concrete floor, lock the door and they go away. Then, competition changes very dramatically. It changes from the competition you ordinarily think of in sports or business, and enters a new realm which I call pure survival. For those of you who have never been there, let me tell you what it's like. When you wake up every morning, you go over to the door of your cell and you either peek under the door or through the cracks or a little hole you have drilled in your door and look outside to see if you can see the sun coming up. If you can see the sun coming up, that means you are still alive. That means you are having a good day.

There was no competition in prison except with the guard outside who had a gun. That wasn't any fun. We did not have any goals. We did not have any direction. We were totally unproductive. All we were trying to do was survive—stay alive for one more day. That's the most difficult environment I have ever dealt with. That is the most wasted feeling I have ever encountered. We lived that way for the first 18 months of imprisonment.

We got lucky in the spring of 1968. The senior ranking officer (SRO) in the camp awoke early one morning and had a brilliant idea as only a senior ranking officer could have. He said, "You know, our physical condition is not too good. Given our circumstances, if the bombers came over tomorrow and blew the walls down, we wouldn't have the strength to walk home." That was probably true! It was 600 miles! He said, "We are going to have a mandatory physical training program." Can you imagine how thrilled we were with that idea? He said "It's not really a big deal, we are just going to ask every man here, without exception, to do 50 push-ups and 50 sit-ups on the first day of the month."

That didn't sound like a very big deal until we tried it. We had to do that on about 300 to 400 calories a day. A small bowl of rice and a small bowl of boiled weeds twice each day was all we ever got to eat. We did not have a lot of steak and eggs in those days. The SRO didn't ask us if we would participate. He said we would. We all saluted smartly and said, "You bet!" and we went off to try. We practiced for a couple of weeks and tried to get ready. A couple of weeks after we started working out, I woke up with my own good idea. I realized that the SRO had just provided us with an opportunity (to excel). He had opened the door to bring some competition back into our lives. The kind we understood. It was something we could do which would take our minds off our more serious problems and at the same time make our lives seem productive again.

PHYSICAL HUMAN POTENTIAL

Two cells away from me there was a very old Navy man. He was about 35 years old and I figured that anybody that old *and* in the Navy couldn't be very tough. I went over to the wall and tapped a message, "How would you like to enter a push-up contest?" He tapped back, "Why not, I'm not going anywhere." He obviously wasn't! The idea was simple. Who can do the most push-ups without stopping? Well, we knew what the rules were. Just to live in our society, we had to do 50 push-ups. If we wanted to win the contest, obviously we would have to do more than that. I worked on the goal for the next few weeks. That was the hardest I had ever worked in my life. I got up on the first day of the month and I did my push-ups. When I finished, I had done 100 push-ups, nonstop. I had never done that before! I never wanted to, as a matter of fact. However, it seemed like something a guy ought to be very proud of so I went over and tapped on the wall, "I'm finished! I did 100 push-ups." He tapped back, "That's not bad for an Air Force officer, I did 150." I thought about that a minute and I said, "Next month, you go first!"

The next month, he went first and I found out an awful lot about old Navy guys. First, they are tougher than they look. Second, they are sneaky! At 5:00 a.m., he woke me up tapping on my wall. He said, "Well, I'm finished. I did 200." I seriously considered staying in bed all day and having a little cry. I had never heard of anybody doing that many push-ups nonstop. I could not imagine how a guy could do that or how I could compete in his world. However, it's absolutely amazing how clear the world gets the minute the goal is established. The goal, if I wanted to win, was to do more than 200 push-ups. I wanted to win so I got up, took a deep breath and did my push-ups. I did 220. I was so proud, I could hardly stand it. I tapped on the wall, "No big deal!" My Navy friend tapped back, "You are right. Don't forget you go first next month." Suddenly I had a new problem–I no longer knew the goal. I did know one thing, it was far more than I wanted to do!

Have you ever tried doing something but been unable to complete the task? That's because you didn't know the goal. It's like having a map with lots of roads but no towns. You can go forever and never arrive at a destination. As Yogi Berra said, "If you don't know where you are going you will probably end up someplace else." I knew where I was going–I was going to win but I didn't know the goal. I did not care what the price might be, I just wanted to win.

You can make no progress toward your goal unless you are willing to change. I decided to change and I made a new commitment; I set my goal and built a plan to conquer this guy. I merely started doing 10 sets of 20 push-ups every day. By the end of the month I was doing 10 sets of 100 every day. I was doing 1,000 push-ups before breakfast! By the way, we didn't get any breakfast, so it didn't interfere! I knew I could beat this guy. On the first day of the next month, I got up and very casually did 300 push-ups nonstop. I guarantee you that is way beyond anything I ever dreamed of doing in my life! It's also possibly more than any of you have ever heard of anyone doing. I could hardly believe it. I crawled across the floor and tapped on the wall and said, "I'm finished! I did 300!" He tapped back and said, "That's not bad for an Air Force officer, I did 660." I didn't want to do that anymore!!

Not being one to give up completely, I tapped to my neighbor, "How would you like to try me in sit-ups?" He said, "You're on!" You know, push-ups are hard work even if you only do one. Sit-ups, on the other hand, are incredibly boring but you can do them all day. My goal was to do so many the first time I would never have to do them again. I set up a program and worked on it for a month. I used the same concept I used for the push-ups, daily incremental improvement, until I achieved the desired result. On the first of the next month, I got up at 5:00 a.m. and started doing sit-ups. I did sit-ups for a little over four hours nonstop. When I finished, I had done 2,000 sit-ups nonstop. Let me provide some perspective on that number. The most I had ever done in my life was 115 when I was in Air Force flying training. In order to graduate and get my wings, I had to do 115 sit-ups nonstop. No one could ever explain to me the correlation between flying and sit-ups, but there must be one. The first time I did 115 sit-ups nonstop I thought I was going to die. What I didn't realize was that with just a little more effort I could have done 2,000. Now I had! I was so proud I couldn't stand it. I couldn't believe anybody on earth could do that. I went over to the wall, tapped and said, "I'm finished. I did 2,000." He said, "Not bad for an Air Force officer! I did 2,700." I didn't want to do that anymore either! In fact, for about a week, I didn't want to do anything that required me to sit up.

I was groping around trying to find some way to compete with this guy, so I tapped on the wall and asked him if he had ever jumped rope before. He said, "I have never done that." I said, "You're on!" When I was 19 years old, I went to Colorado to put on a ski demonstration. I had never skied before in my life, but a friend of mine told me over the phone how to do it. He said, "It's easy! Rent boots and skis, go to the top and come down!" In those days I really believed things were that easy. So I went to Colorado to the 12,000 foot peak of Loveland Basin, put on my skis and started down the mountain. Thirty minutes later I had broken my leg in four different places. I wore a long leg cast for about five months. My therapy to learn to walk again was to jump rope. Therefore, I had jumped rope a lot. I knew how to do that very well. So I challenged the Navy guy to a jump rope contest. Simply put, the one who jumps rope the most times without missing is the winner.

We took an old shirt, tore it up into little strips and braided them into a rope to start the contest. It lasted about four and a half years. When we first started, we were pretty amateurish. We would do 30, 40 maybe even 60 jumps on a good day. Then we would miss and have to start over. By the end of the war, in March of 1973, when I was released from prison, I held the world record, 3,640 times over the rope without missing. In fairness to the Navy guy, I have to tell you a secret. The day he was released from prison he held the world record, but unfortunately, he was released from prison 20 days before me. That left 20 days more before the contest was over. One of the things we learned in prison was that if you had to cheat to win, then go ahead and cheat! I merely waited until he went home–I knew he wasn't going to give up–and I finished him off. When I got home, I mailed him a note which said, "You lose!"

The number of times you can jump rope, or do sit-ups and push-ups are entertaining things to talk about and laugh about and they lead to the real lesson which came right near the end of the war. In late 1972, I lived with a young Navy man. One day I was down on the floor knocking out my push-ups. He came by and said, "I'm really impressed! I would love to be able to do 100 push-ups." I said, "You can, just do everything I tell you for the next 30 days and I promise to teach you to do that." He asked, "How do I start?" "How many can you do?" I responded. "I can do 10." "Well," I suggested, "that's not great, but you have to start somewhere. Let's see you do it." He did, and I walked around the cell a couple of times and said, "Let's see you do that again." Each time I went by his bunk that day he had to do 10 push-ups. Each time I went by the next day, he had to do 12. I was going to use the same philosophy with him I had used on myself, daily incremental improvement.

By the beginning of the third day it was becoming apparent he was not going to make it at the rate we were going. He was working too hard. I told him, "Charlie, I tell you what, you're working too hard for the amount you are getting back, so let me do half the work for you. You do the push-ups and I'll count them for you." He's a Navy guy, he signed up. One great quality of Navy guys is that they will try anything. He asked what he should do and I told him, "Get on the floor and start pushing. I'll start talking to you so you don't get bored and I'll count for you and I'll tell you when you are finished." When I got through counting that day he had done 100 push-ups nonstop. It didn't take thirty days, it only took three days. The real truth is he could have done it the first day, but he didn't believe it and he wasn't willing to try. The real truth is that with few exceptions everyone who reads this book could do 100 push-ups today just like that if you believed it and were willing to try.

You wonder what human potential is? We have no clue. It's way beyond anything you have ever done. If you believe in yourself as much as we did and are willing to expend that level of effort each day of your life, your capacity far exceeds what you have done in your life. Physical capability is not fundamentally different than the quality performance we desire from each individual. It's there. You were born with the ability, but we can't buy it from you, nor can we beat it out of you. We only get it when you decide to put out. You can only do that when you decide to do it. If you are a leader, or aspire to be a leader, your greatest challenge will be to create an atmosphere where people want to produce at that level.

MENTAL HUMAN POTENTIAL

You may be wondering what else we learned while hanging around in Hanoi. Yes, we learned that physical condition is a very, very important part of our lives while we were imprisoned. But, there is another part of our lives which is even more critical. It's called mental condition. Mental health in prison is probably the most difficult issue one has to deal with in captivity. Some of you may not be old enough to remember the Vietnam War, and among those who are, many view it as a totally negative event. For the benefit of everyone, let me divide the war into smaller bite-sized chunks so you can swallow it. September 1969 would be pretty close to the mid-point of the war from our perspective. I called the period prior to 1969, the period of stark terror. In my case, it lasted three years and three months. I have already told you what that's like, where you wake up in the morning and look outside to see if you can see the sun rising. If you see it, you know you are alive and having a good day. During this time, keeping our minds occupied was very simple. The guard outside had a gun. If you got bored, you merely told him and he could make life very exciting, in a heartbeat!

In September of 1969, a lot of things happened. We didn't know what all of them meant, but we immediately appreciated the result. The way we were treated dramatically improved. We entered a new era, a period I call the doldrums. Basically it was three and a half years with no place to go, nothing to do, and nobody harassing us. It seemed like a good deal compared to where we had been. But let me tell you what happened. The minute we entered into that period, we ran into a level of boredom that we could not comprehend. One of the things you have to understand is that we didn't have any books, and we didn't have any pencils or paper. We had *nothing* in that cell. We had memorized everything that happened in the world for three and a half years. That had always been enough to occupy our minds.

Now that they took the harassment away, we had about a thousand percent increase in the amount of time on our hands. We couldn't begin to fill that time. We had been memorizing information forever. Now we didn't have enough and that was a very serious concern. We weren't sure we would survive mentally under those circumstances. We put the word out to everybody in every building and said, "If anybody here knows anything we don't know, pass it to us and we promise you we will memorize it. You can send us the names of all your dogs, or all your wives or anything you can think of, even if it's junk information, and we will memorize it."

Two days after we started, a message came to us from a man two cells away and he said, "When I was a young boy I had a very unusual experience which may become beneficial to us. When I was only 10 years old, my mother taught high school English. Every Monday morning she would give me a poem to learn. I would work on it all week. Friday night at the family dinner I was allowed to recite that poem to my whole family. If I did well I got to eat. I learned a lot of poetry over the years." His favorite works were by Kipling. He had learned works like *Gunga Din*, *The Ballad of East and West*, *If*, and a variety of other poems. He said, "Let me think about that for a couple of days. If I can remember any of those poems, I'll pass them on to you and you can all learn them." We just hung around the house for the next few days waiting for this guy to entertain us. Finally he came over and tapped on the wall and said, "Let's start with *The Ballad of East and West.*"

You may have heard it. It starts out, "*Oh, East is East, and West is West, and never the twain shall meet.*" That's the first line of the poem. That's the part I knew. That is the first line of the first verse; there are actually 46 verses, as we learned it.

This guy thought he could remember all the verses. He said, "I'll tell you what we'll do. I'll send you a verse every day until you memorize the whole poem." Each day for the next 44 days, he would tap on the wall first thing in the morning and give us the next verse. We were memorizing and doing pretty well, but on the 45th day, he didn't tap on the wall. Nobody knew why. Sometimes in prison we didn't want to do anything. Nobody harassed us when we didn't want to do anything. On the 46th day he didn't tap on the wall either, and that bothered me so I went over and said, "Hey Norm, do you mind telling us how this story ends?" He was very reluctant but he finally came over and said, "You're not going to believe this, but I can't remember the last two verses!" Have you ever read a book and come to the end and someone has stolen the last page? It sounds trivial, stupid, almost. But as I look back on it, that is the second most frustrating situation we had during the entire period of time we were imprisoned. The most frustrating experience occurred in the Spring of 1968 when President Johnson stopped the bombing. Everybody assumed we would be home free in the next 90 days. Five years later, we were still there. That was serious frustration.

A year and a half after Johnson stopped the bombing, in late 1969, we learned 44 verses of a 46 verse poem. But we didn't know how it ended and we had no way to find out. We were horribly depressed. We sat around the cell staring at the walls. About the third day, Norm came over and tapped on the wall. He was very excited. He tapped, "You guys are in luck! I found the missing verses. You are not going to believe this. You are not missing the last two verses, you already have them! You are missing verse 12 and verse 26! I left them out. It's no big deal! Just put them in the right place and you will have the whole poem." I am here to tell you, it *is* a big deal. You want to try something tough? Go out and learn yourself a long poem, shuffle the verses and try to learn the poem again. That is not a small task. But we took it seriously, and eventually mastered the poem.

When we were released from the prison three and a half years later, the first thing we all did was to go to the library and look up the poem. We wanted to check this guy's sincerity. We trusted no one! We wanted to see if he was lying! The poem we learned was virtually word perfect. The most amazing part of this story was that before Norm taught us the 46 verses, he had not thought about that poem for 25 years. I am convinced that all the information that you have ever been exposed to, through reading, hearing, or seeing, is stored in your memory. If you believe that and if you believe it's feasible to reach in and grope around and retrieve it as we did, then all of your stored information is available to you. The potential of the human mind is so great, so far beyond the realm of what we have explored, that we had great difficulty comprehending the totality of what we had discovered. The challenge is to believe and be willing to exert the effort even when the effort required is monumental.

Let's shift gears here for a moment. You have read that we tapped on the walls to each other. Unless you have been to jail lately you probably won't know why we tapped. When you go to prison, the first thing the guards do is give you a long list of rules to learn. They are not like anything you have ever seen and are not rules that you would have any interest in. The very first rule in Hanoi was written on the wall; they would never allow you to forget it: "You are not allowed to make any sound that can be heard outside your cell." That means that if you are in solitary confinement, you don't talk to anybody. Since the day you were born, people have been trying to convince you, through a variety of courses, how important communications are in your life. If you want to confirm this, spend a few days locked in prison 10,000 miles from home. You'll quickly discover how important communication is when you have nobody to talk to.

For us to survive in that environment, it was important for us to have a way to communicate, but communicating with one another was against the rules. We were lucky because one of the first people captured in North Vietnam had read a book one time that described a universal tap code used in prisons throughout the world. He remembered how the code worked and thought it would be valuable to share the information. I was lucky enough to learn the code my very first week in captivity. I was being interrogated shortly after I arrived. I was sitting on a little wooden stool in the middle of the floor. Every time I would answer the interrogator's question, he would smile and show his approval. If I didn't answer, he would knock me to the floor. Since both hands were tied behind my back, each time the guard knocked me off the stool, my head hit the floor. About the fourth time he knocked me off the stool, I suddenly got a whole lot smarter. I decided that if a guy stayed on the floor, he wouldn't have very far to fall. I didn't have a plan—no clue. I just didn't want to get up only to be knocked down again. So I just lay there. The interrogator talked to me about that for a while and then he kicked me in the head a couple of times and became bored and left.

The minute he went out the door, I ransacked his desk. In the third drawer I opened I found a message written right on the wood in ink. Some American had already been there. It said, "All American POW's Learn This Code: C=K, tap down and across. Good Luck."

Directly beneath the writing the POW had drawn a matrix similar to the one below.

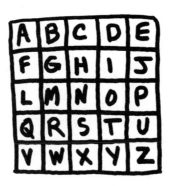

Already in the
cockpit at age six.

My first day in the
Air Force Reserve -
24 Jun 55.

Upon completion of Jungle Survival
School, Clark Air Base, Philippine
Islands - 19 Jun 66.

The night before my
airplane was shot
down -
19 Jul 66.

I was shot down
in an aircraft
similar to these -
20 Jul 66.

Mr. & Mrs. Jess E. Hubbard
5242 Delmar
Shawnee Mission, Kans

It is with deep regret that I officially inform you that your son
1st Lt Edward L. Hubbard has been missing in action since 20 Jul 66
over North Viet Nam. Your son was a navigator of an RB-66 aircraft
on an operational mission. The flight was normal to the target area.
Aircraft was apparently hit by surface to air missile while orbiting
over the target area. Aircraft descended and was observed to disinte-
grate. Two parachutes were cited but no beepers were heard. Other
aircraft stayed in the area until fuel ran low and search had to be
discontinued due to hostile location. It is possible that your son
could have been taken captive by hostile forces because of the area
in which he is missing. If this is true it is suggested that in reply
to inquiries from sources outside your immediate family, for his
welfare, you reveal only his name, rank, service number and date of
birth. This is the same information he must provide his possible
captors. If further information is received you will be notified
immediately. Should you desire information you may contact my duty
officer at area code 512 Olive 8-5311 Ext 3805. Please accept my
sincere sympathy in this time of anxiety.

Major General G. B. Greene Jr
Assistant Deputy Chief of Staff
Personnel, for Military Personnel
Headquarters, United States Air Force

Letter from the Air Force informing my parents
that I was missing in action. Hand delivered by
officers from Richards-Gebaur AFB - 21 Jul 66.

BU46 NS SNA491 XV GOVT CAS PD 10 EXTRA MSC RANDOLPH AFB

TEX 10 FEB 434 P CST

MR AND MRS JESS E HUBBARD RPT DLY

     5242 DELMAR SHAWNEE MISSION KANS

IT IS MY EXTREME PLEASURE TO INFORM YOU THAT WE HAVE THIS DATE
CHANGED THE STATUS OF YOUR SON, CAPTAIN EDWARD L HUBBARD,
FROM MISSING IN ACTION TO CAPTURED. TO INSURE HIS WELFARE,
IT IS REQUESTED THAT YOU PROVIDE ONLY HIS NAME, RANK, SERVICE
NUMBER AND DATE OF BIRTH IN ANSWER TO INQUIRIES FROM SOURCES
OUTSIDE YOUR IMMEDIATE FAMILY. THE INFORMATION CHANGING HIS
STATUS FROM MISSING IN ACTION TO CAPTURED WILL BE MADE PUBLIC
IN ROUTING DEPARTMENT OF DEFENSE INFORMATION RELEASES. THIS
ANNOUNCEMENT WILL BE LIMITED TO CHANGE IN STATUS. INFORMATION
AVAILABLE TO US INDICATES THAT THOSE BEING HELD BY THE NORTH
VIETNAMESE ARE RECEIVING ADEQUATE CARE AND ARE BEING HUMANELY
TREATED. CONTINUING EFFORTS ARE BEING EXERTED BY OUR STATE
DEPARTMENT TO GAIN ADDITIONAL INFORMATION ABOUT OUR PERSONNEL
AND TO EFFECT A PRISONER EXCHANGE. AGAIN, BE ASSURED THAT ANY
NEW INFORMATION WE RECEIVE WILL BE FURNISHED IMMEDIATELY.

        LT. COLONEL JOSEPH G LUTHER CHIEF
        CASUALTY DIVISION DIRECTORATE OF PERSONNEL SERVICES
              HEADQUARTERS
        UNITED STATES AIR FORCE

        532P CST

Telegram to my parents changing my status
from missing in action to captured -
10 Feb 67.

North Vietnamese
propaganda photo
excerpted from "Pilots
in Pajamas," an East
German movie made in
Hanoi - 28 Jun 67.

"Welcome to Freedom." My first handshake
as a free man -
Hanoi, 4 Mar 73.

John Witt's life-size oil painting of me hangs in the Pentagon - 22 Mar 83.

My induction as Honorary Chief Master Sergeant - Sep 88.

Speaking at Fort Benning awards
ceremony on POW-MIA Day -
Sep 89.

With Jennifer, my wife, at my
retirement ceremony on my last
day in the Air Force - 1 Aug 90.

As President of my own company, Positive
Vectors, providing motivation and inspiration at
Harris Corporation's Annual Quality Awards
Ceremony in Melbourne, Fl - 91.

It was a very simple code, not like Morse Code, which has no apparent rhyme or reason. If you forget the appropriate dots and dashes for any letter in Morse Code, there is no way to go back and reconstruct it. On the other hand, with the tap code, you will never forget. However, the tap code was cumbersome because it took so long to spell out each word. But this presented no problem for your average American.

Have you any idea what Americans do best? We always find a better, simpler way to do things. We abbreviated the entire English language. One of the advantages of being in the military is that we hardly ever use words anyway. We use mostly abbreviations and acronyms. This custom came to our rescue in prison. The letter *N* came to stand for *and*. The only people who know how long it takes to type the word *and* are guys tapping on the wall, or secretaries typing it all day. So we reduced it to one letter. We reduced the whole language to two- or three-letter words. My favorite word in the whole vocabulary that we evolved was the letter *Q*, which stood for *quiz*. Quiz is a four-letter word fighter pilots use in place of the word interrogation because fighter pilots can't spell the word interrogation.

The word we used the most was represented by the letter *c* which stood for the word *clear*. It was against the rules to communicate. If we were caught communicating, there was big trouble. If we got caught in enough trouble in prison, we could really get hurt seriously. We believe two Americans lost their lives simply because they got caught in a communications purge. A communications purge was severe punishment heaped on prisoners usually when someone was caught communicating. It was a rather serious thing. We spent eight to ten hours a day lying on the floor peeking under the door or through a little hole in the wall, to make sure no guard was around when we were trying to communicate. When we tapped *c* on the wall everybody knew it was safe to communicate. It was an important part of life.

On Sunday morning about 10:00 a.m. we would hear a loud thumping on the wall (TAP...TAP TAP TAP). This *C* stood for *church call*. The senior-ranking American had decided it was time for everyone to go to church. Church in prison is probably a little different than anything you have been to before. There, it made no difference what religion you were or if you had any religion at all. Somewhere around 10:00 a.m. on Sunday morning, whether you lived by yourself or with 100 people, we stopped what we were doing and sat down and honored church call at the same time and essentially in the same way. It was done for two reasons. For all the people who were religious, it had an obvious meaning. For every single American who was there, religious or otherwise, it was the one time each week when every single man was rowing the boat in exactly the same direction at the same time. The strength we derived from that unity of effort was absolutely awesome. That's what we held on to. That is called teamwork and it is the most valuable and yet most underrated and under utilized concept in our nation. Ironically, it is *free!*

Try to remember the last time you saw a group of Americans pulling together–except in time of crisis. Can you imagine what would happen if everybody who reads this book would row the boat in exactly the same direction for just one day? Pulling together–everybody going in the same direction. If we could ever do that for one day in this country we could solve the drug problem. If we are ever going to solve any of the serious problems facing our nation, we must learn to pull together.

Late in the prison day, we heard the tapping of a *G* and an *N*. That stands for *good night*. We say good night to people all of our lives. Why would we stop just because we went to prison? It's one of the small pleasantries in life that seems insignificant but takes on a greater meaning at times like that.

Late in 1968, I lived next to an empty cell. At about 9:00 p.m. that night the guards put an American in that cell, locked the door, and went away. The minute the coast was clear, I tapped good night to this guy. He tapped back and said, "Thank you very much. You are the first guy I have talked to for three years." That's how important tapping *G N* became some days.

The very last thing we did every night was to tap out *GBA–God Bless America*. Every American there tapped that on the wall to the guy next door to him each night of captivity. That was to make sure nobody ever forgot why we were there and that no one ever forgot how important it was to perform to the best of his ability every single day. Performing to the best of your ability was a life and death matter. In our society, it could also become a life and death matter if we don't learn to give it our best every day.

I am frequently asked what we did with the tap code after we learned it. First thing, we tapped on the wall to the guy next to us to find out what his name was. We kept track of every person who was there. We knew the name of every person in every cell in the whole camp. I was moved 37 times and I was never in a cell more than an hour or two before I knew the name and location of every person in the camp. The information became a very important part of our lives.

In late 1969, as conditions improved, we expanded our horizons. We began looking for things to do so we started an education program. Right after the education program started, I moved in next door to a man named Everett Alvarez. Alvie was the very first person captured in North Vietnam on the 5th of August, 1964.

When I had been in prison two weeks, Alvarez had already been there two years! By the time I moved in next to him, he had been there five years. He was an amazing guy. He never, ever lost sight of the important things in life. He never lost sight of the value of maintaining his sense of humor, no matter how tricky things became. I lived next to him for eighteen months, and every single morning at 5:00 a.m. the first sound I heard was Alvarez tapping a joke on the wall to me. I know he made those jokes up. They have to be the worst jokes I have ever heard. But the very fact that this man could still think that there was something funny left in this world after five years in that place became quite an inspiration to all of us. If it was funny to him, then by God, it had better be funny to the rest of us. We all tried and we all gained from that experience.

Another thing that was pretty impressive about Alvie was that he was one of those people I mentioned earlier who remembered all the things he learned in his life. He remembered everything. He grew up in a neighborhood where Spanish was a second language so he was fluent in it. I grew up in Kansas City. We don't do a lot of Spanish in Kansas City, so I didn't know any Spanish. During the period of time I lived next to him, I used to tap on the wall about eight hours every day in English and he would tap to me in Spanish. After 18 months of living next to Alvarez, I had a 5,000-word vocabulary in Spanish. I was fluent in a foreign language that I had never seen written and never heard spoken. All I ever heard was Alvie tapping on the wall. Later, I moved to the other end of the camp to a cell with 37 people. Nobody spoke Spanish. Logically, I became the Spanish teacher. I taught Spanish the last three and a half years of the war.

I had never been to college in my life, so when I came home in 1973 it looked like time to go. My first order of business was to sign up for a night school course in Spanish. The first night of class I walked in the door, took the final exam and maxed the course never having opened the book. You wonder what human potential is mentally? We haven't a clue! It is way beyond anything you have ever tried. When I first told that story, shortly after my release, a lady in the audience came forward and challenged my story. She said, "You know the story about learning Spanish? I don't believe that!" I simply responded, "If you didn't believe that, then you probably won't believe this either. I don't even care!" She was embarrassed and said she didn't mean to sound so skeptical. She thought it was a neat story, but hard to believe. She told me that if I could convince her, she would like to pass the story on to others. I agreed to try.

I told her about my experience of living in France and observing that almost all of the four and five-year old American children became fluent in French because of their exposure to the French workers on the base. The reason they were able to do that was because, just like all of you reading this, they were born with the ability. Fortunately, they had not yet reached the age when their parents told them it was too difficult. They didn't know any better. They just did it! One of the great tragedies of our society is that adults spend every waking moment telling children what they can't do, and rarely point out what they *can* do. The result should be anticipated—that children will grow up doubting their own abilities and that their performance will suffer. In prison, we were just like those children in France. No one told us that what we were trying to do was too hard to do, so we just did it! The skeptical lady agreed that this was a very clever story. I told her if she thought that was clever, she would love my next story.

A man who came home the same time I did was less fortunate than I. I came back and was medically grounded for one year and then I flew F-4s for 12 years. This man came back and was medically grounded and NEVER got to fly again. He went off to Texas to get another degree. The first week he was in Texas he quizzed out 48 hours of college credit in four foreign languages: Spanish, German, French and Russian. He has never seen the books in his life–ever! He learned four foreign languages by tapping on the wall of a North Vietnamese prison with some other American who had read the book.

In the cell where I taught my Spanish, there were many fascinating characters. I would like to share some information about two particular individuals because I believe these stories speak volumes about human mental capacity.

The first was the very first American with whom I communicated via the tap code, but a man whom I would not meet face-to-face for another four and one-half years. Jim is a man I will never forget for a couple of reasons. First, during my initial contact with Jim in July 1966, he told me very authoritatively that the war would be over 90 days after the first bombing of Hanoi. Since the first bombing of Hanoi had occurred three weeks prior to my capture, it was apparent that my captivity was going to be abbreviated. So, I calmly tapped on the wall and said, "I think I can do this standing on my head." As a visionary, Jim would have made a good coal miner–he missed his prediction by almost six and a half years. When I finally met Jim face-to-face, over four years later, my first comment was, "The top of my head is certainly getting sore!" He knew precisely what I meant. What Jim lacked in his ability to foresee the future was more than compensated for by his incredible mind and his ability to educate and entertain his fellow prisoners.

Many of Jim's early years were spent in Great Britain. I will never forget his great story about a return trip to the United States aboard a ship. Jim had depicted the trip in an excellent drawing on the bottom of his bed board using a piece of broken brick. (One must understand the quality of Vietnamese bricks. They were quite soft and made good chalk.) His was a picture of a young lad in short pants leaning over the rail, and as Jim put it, "feeding his already digested lunch to the fish."

This was only one of hundreds of humorous stories which complemented Jim's drawings. They were all part of the classes he taught us when the North Vietnamese guards weren't looking. Jim was fluent in French and German and his drawings were the focus of whatever story he was currently teaching. The reason the drawings were done on the bottom of his bed board was that we weren't allowed to draw, or hold classes, or do much of anything else. None of which bothered Jim.

I was quite fascinated by this man who seemed to have endless talent. However, his language classes, complete with pictures, paled by comparison to some of his other performances. In mid-1971 he proudly announced that he would soon finish the first of the books he was writing–in his head! He was going to call this the *Color Trilogy* and the first book would be *The Red Kite*. Jim asked if we would be interested in hearing his story. In a world with nothing to do and no place to go, 24 hours a day, 365 days a year, we were interested in anything that would pass some time. Little did we know what an extraordinary experience we were about to enjoy. Jim said he would tell us one chapter of his book each day. He didn't just give us a synopsis of each chapter. He told the story in amazing detail, complete with all the dialogue. If you closed your eyes, you believed he was actually reading from a book.

Even more astounding than hearing Jim's story the first time, was hearing it the second time, two and a half years later in a different cell, in a different camp, with a different group of POWs. To the very best of my recollection, it was virtually verbatim to the first time. I will remember *The Red Kite* as well as any published novel I will ever read. *The Red Kite* was only the first. Next came Jim's adventure story, *The White Goat.* It was a story about the British soldiers and the problems they faced in the Himalayan mountains prior to the independence of India.

The third story, and without a doubt the most interesting, was *A Twist of Lemon*, which was set in London during World War II and described the trials and tribulations of a young English lass who fell in love with a Yank. When it came time for Jim to tell us the last chapter he offered us an interesting dilemma. He had composed two last chapters, a happy ending and a sad ending. We had to choose which we wanted! It was a fascinating study in human psychology. Given our circumstances–everyone in the cell had been in captivity more than six years–what would they choose? What would you have chosen? Jim offered yet another option, no last chapter. He would leave it to our imaginations. Eventually, we heard both endings and as you might have guessed, everyone preferred the happy ending. It did, however, lead us into a very lengthy discussion (turned argument) concerning the realism of "They all lived happily ever after." At the time, we weren't all that certain of a happy ending. Now, more than 20 years later, those of us who survived to return home surely must believe in happy endings.

We were certainly intrigued and entertained by Jim's ability to write a good book. However, by comparison, I believe we were all absolutely overwhelmed by another cell mate who appeared to have read every book ever written. Even more astounding, he remembered them!

In November 1970, following the unsuccessful attempt to liberate American POWs at Son Tay, all Americans were moved to the infamous Hanoi Hilton. I had the privilege of moving into the section of the Hilton known as Camp Unity, and more specifically into Cell #1. For the first time in our captivity we were living in large groups. There were 59 POWs in Cell #1. Among the men I met in Cell #1 was an interesting gent named Dave, who was a graduate of West Point. Though he was a highly qualified officer, being promoted well ahead of his contemporaries, and also a pilot of some renown, he had a more important trait–he was a scholar. That fact would become evident and very important in the next two years.

Following a major flap between the North Vietnamese guards and the ever-demanding American POWs, yet another shuffle ensued. Thirty-seven of us, including Dave, ended up in Cell #5 across the camp. We now had a bit more space, so we settled in and decided to get organized. It just so happened that I was one of only four men in the cell who had not yet been to college. I recognized a great opportunity for us "dummies" to pick the brains of all the college grads. I volunteered to establish an education program. One of the benefits of "Ed's Ed Program" was the previously discussed *Color Trilogy*. In addition, there were classes in language, math, physics, anatomy and even an

Arthur Murray dance class. But, I think I can safely say nothing drew a larger attendance, nor more rave reviews, than Dave's World Literature course.

Dave was a lit major, had a Master's Degree in literature, and had taught literature for many years at the Air Force Academy. When I initially approached him about providing a lit course for "Ed's Ed" he didn't seem particularly excited about the idea, but did promise to give it some thought. I mentioned it several more times over the next two weeks and he gave me a rather halfhearted, "I'm working on it." Little did I know what was going on in Dave's amazing mind. Soon I would find out!

Out of the clear blue sky, Dave approached me one day and said, "I am ready to propose a literature class schedule for you. I am prepared to teach a two-hour session five nights each week." I was dumbfounded, but told him there was no need to hurry through the course–we would probably be around for awhile. Dave assured me he had sufficient material (in his head) to sustain that level of effort for several years. He was correct!

His class was structured in the following manner: on the first night he provided a two-hour biographical sketch of an author; on the second night he explained how the different aspects of life affected the author's personal style of writing; and on the third night, Dave summarized one or more works written by that particular author. Dave started with Moses! When I was moved 18 months later, Dave was still going strong. He had progressed to discussing 20th Century authors, but showed no signs of running short of information. Dave's literature class may well be the singularly most astounding demonstration of human mental potential I will ever witness. At the same time, I would not want to leave you with the impression that only one or two people demonstrated this unusual mental capacity. Just within this one cell, as part of "Ed's Ed," we had Larry's four-year college equivalent math class, Charlie's physics, Bill's anatomy, George's French, and Jim's French and German classes.

If you ever have the opportunity that we had to go back and review your life and all your accomplishments, please take it. This review will become one of the most valuable experiences of your life. Look at what you have tried. Some attempts have been unsuccessful. Forget them; they are not critical. Concentrate on your triumphs, the foundation for your future. Among those accomplishments, a few will stand out in your mind–the things that mean the most to you will invariably be your accomplishments under adverse circumstances. That is where we all perform our very best. It was no different in prison. The only difference was that we measured adversity using a slightly different yardstick.

We learned a whole lot about human potential, both physically and mentally, while we hung around prison. All of our experiences occurred under the tremendous duress of captivity. The examples and lessons recounted thus far were, by our prison standards, simple ones. I assure you, there were many other lessons which were not at all simple. As I said, our yardsticks were different.

HOLD ON

Earlier I mentioned I was not going to waste your time telling you a lot of horror stories, and I don't plan to do that. I want to tell you one brief story about adverse circumstances because I think it will help you understand more clearly what's really, truly available to you as a human being, both physically and mentally, when the chips are down. *If*, by Rudyard Kipling, one of the poems we learned, has several verses that apply to this situation I'm going to describe to you. The verses are:

> If you can force your heart and nerve and sinew
> To serve your turn long after they are gone,
> And so hold on when there is nothing in you
> Except the Will which says to them: "Hold On!"

I am going to tell you what it means to hold on according to one man's standards. This is a story about a man who understands that poem so well he could have written it. About midnight on May 9, 1969, two men escaped from the camp where we lived. They went over the wall and into downtown Hanoi. They walked around most of the night, and about 5:00 a.m. they were captured and brought back. By the time the sun went down that day, one of those men had already been beaten to death. This was a very, very serious business we were involved in. You could lose your life in an instant if you made a mistake. This guy made a mistake. Anytime we broke the rules there was a purge and this purge was different only in that it was probably the worst purge we ever had. They took the senior ranking man from every building in camp, 16 men, took everything they owned, tied them up and put them in solitary confinement and started beating them. The beatings went on for an extended period of time. The North Vietnamese wanted to know who knew about the escape, what the plan was, and if we had collaborators on the outside. Because none of these 16 men was particularly interested in discussing those subjects with them, the beatings continued for some time.

Eventually, the North Vietnamese guards got tired of the program and they took 15 of these men and put them back in the system and took one man and isolated him. They decided they could get everything they needed from this individual. To truly understand and appreciate what that man went through you would really have to know him. Basically, he was a man from the deep South, and if you have ever met a true Southerner, you know that they walk much slower than the average person. They talk so slow you always want to help them finish their sentences. But they have a neat quality that folks from the North don't have. People from the South rarely get upset about things. We call them easy goin'. That's the kind of person this man was. He was very humble almost to an extreme. He was nearly apologetic. When he was being interrogated he would say, "I'm sorry, I can't answer your questions." He stuck with that for about a week and then he got sick of that. The next time he was taken to be interrogated that afternoon he told them, "You know, I have told you that I'm not going to answer your questions, but today I want to tell you something you have never heard before." The interrogators became excited. They thought they had finally broken this man. He continued, "Starting right now, I am never going to speak to you again." He refused to talk to them. Nobody knows why he made that decision but it was certainly gutsy. We gave him very high marks in courage, but perhaps slightly lower marks in judgment.

The Vietnamese were totally unimpressed. They merely marched him into a cell, put him down on his hands and knees on the concrete floor, and said, "You have had a tough week. Now we are going to let you rest. From 9:00 p.m. tonight until 5:00 a.m. tomorrow morning you are allowed to stay right there on your hands and knees. You can even sleep there if you want. But from 5:00 a.m. tomorrow morning to 9:00 p.m. tomorrow night you'll stay there on your knees and hold your hands over your head and you are going to do that every day from now on." Have you ever tried that before? Someday, when you are bored, get on your knees and put your hands over your head and see how long you like that game. It won't take very long. The first thing that happens when you put your hands up is that your back hurts. Shortly after that your arms hurt. Shortly after that you put your arms down. There is a slight difference when you are in prison. When you put your arms down, the guy standing behind you has a rubber hose and he rips you across the back to get your attention. It's absolutely guaranteed to work. It leaves a welt about three inches wide all across your back that lasts about six to eight weeks and causes excruciating pain. This guy was getting hit with the rubber hose about 100 times a day. Still, he refused to talk to them.

They continued that treatment for a while and then they got tired of clowning around so they decided to get serious. They took him out and tied him up into a little ball and hung him up. They did everything they knew how to do and in the process they broke his left arm. They continued to beat this guy and he resolutely refused to talk to them. They did that for several days and then they put him back to rest again. He was allowed to rest on his hands and knees at night and hold his hands in the air during the day. He did that for 14 consecutive days, with a broken arm and little or no sleep. He never talked to them. We don't know what happened on the 14th day. All I know is that I was at my favorite location, down on my knees by my door. I had drilled a tiny hole and I could see the courtyard. About 5:00 p.m. that evening they dragged this man's body into the courtyard right in front of me. He was about 10 to 15 feet away from me so I got a good look at him. Based on his physical appearance, one would have to assume that he was dead, except for one thing. That guy had gotten up and was still able to walk on his own power. He was still holding his head up. He understood what Kipling was talking about. *"If you can force your heart and nerve and sinew To serve your turn long after they are gone, And so hold on when there is nothing left in you except the Will which says to them: 'Hold on!'"* That man knows more about holding on than any of us will ever know.

I have told that story to several hundred thousand people over the last few years. Without exception, everybody says, "God! I'm glad I wasn't there. I would never be able to hold on." The most important thing I am going to tell you in this entire book is that you are wrong. Nobody was handpicked to go to prison in North Vietnam. Nobody volunteered to go to prison in North Vietnam. Every one of us got there by accident. We represented a cross-section of the American public just as you do. There is only one very small difference between you and us. We were there, we didn't have any choice, so we did whatever it took to stay alive. Because you weren't there, because you don't have the privilege of that kind of experience it's probably a little tricky to sit in your comfortable surroundings and try to figure out what you would do, what you could reach out to and hold on to for up to nine and a half years to stay alive in that environment.

For you to understand what's available to you as a human being, what's really truly possible, it's very important for you to understand where we have been, what we did, why it worked so well for us, and why it would work for everyone of you if you had been there. The only way I know to get you closer to understanding that is to put you through a little exercise which takes just a few minutes. Let me describe a day in solitary confinement. I describe the situation as "my place." When I give a speech, I have people close their eyes and visualize and feel just a little bit of what I saw and felt. For purposes of this book, if you must read the words yourself, you will just have to exercise your imagination a bit more. Or, you can have someone read you the words so that you achieve the full effect audiences receive during a speech. I hope when you complete the exercise, the meaning of everything I have described will be much clearer and your appreciation for your own untapped potential will be far greater.

My place was a little cell that I referred to earlier. This particular cell was in the camp we called the Zoo located on the outskirts of Hanoi. The cell was affectionately known among the prisoners as the Outhouse. The time for me was December 1966. I had been in prison about five months and I had been in solitary confinement in the Outhouse for the preceding 28 days. I couldn't see in those days, partly because I didn't have a window, but mostly because both my eyes were completely swollen shut from being beaten in the face every day for the past 28 days. I could not hear in those days either, with the exception of a strange thumping noise. I had never heard that noise in my entire life and it took me four or five days to figure out that it was my heartbeat. That throbbing sound was all I could hear because both my eardrums were broken.

Less than five feet from where I spent my life in those days, where I ate and diagonally across the cell from where I slept in the corner, was a little rusty bucket which served as my latrine. The smell from that bucket was absolutely unbelievable. That wasn't particularly important. What was important was the fact that the bucket only had a one-day capacity. Because I had been in a reasonable amount of trouble, I had not been allowed to go out and empty that bucket for the last 10 days. The only option available to me was to dip the contents of the bucket and pour them through a tiny hole in the wall of my cell. I had to do this with the soup bowl from which I ate. There was no way to wash the bowl. I slept on a concrete floor in those days.

The temperature outside was 20 degrees. The temperature of the concrete was 20 degrees. I hadn't had a bath for 28 days and I have never been so filthy in all my life. My morale has never been that low before or since.

I wasn't overly concerned about the small amount of rations or the cold. I was concerned with something that never crossed my mind before. Would I still be alive on New Year's Day? That was exactly three days away. TAP ... TAP TAP TAP, When I heard that sound, I suddenly remembered it was Sunday again. Even though I had been completely separated from everyone in the camp for 28 days, I never lost sight of the value and importance of attending church call with everybody else. I have told you that church in prison is probably a little bit different than any church you have ever been to. Our program always started with "I Pledge Allegiance to the Flag of The United States of America..." which we did with greater sincerity than anything we had ever done in our lives.

Depending on where you lived, the program varied, but usually the next thing was the Twenty-third Psalm. There were a couple of lines that seemed to be written for us. One of those lines says, "Yea, though I walk through the valley of the shadow of death, I will fear no evil..." The single most important lesson we learned in prison was that fear is nothing more than a feeling that comes over you when you lack confidence in your ability to cope with life as it has been dealt to you. Once you step up and accept full responsibility for your own future and your own fate, and once you step up and find out how simple it is to cope with life, fear is not such a big deal anymore.

The other line says, "Thou preparest a table before me in the presence of mine enemies...my cup runneth over." This was certainly the most ironic situation we had ever been in during our lives: locked up, ten thousand miles from home, all by ourselves, giving thanks every day for our good fortune. You see, those of us who were locked up behind bars were actually the free people in that prison. The men on the outside with the guns and the keys are still there. Those people have been imprisoned for life because their minds have been captured. Ours are still free. We always finished our church service in prison by singing "God Bless America." We sang it rather quietly in those days because the last thing we needed to do was to get into any more trouble.

Now I would like you to do something today that you may not have done for a long time, maybe something that you have never done before in your life. I would like you to sing, "God Bless America." If you are alone, sing it alone. If you are with others, explain what you are reading, and ask them to join you. You might be amazed at how it makes you feel. You might feel a chill up your spine or a lump in your throat. That, ladies and gentlemen, is pride in being an American. And that, ladies and gentlemen, is pride in doing the very best in everything you do in life. That, ladies and gentlemen is exactly what we felt all day, every day for five, six, seven and up to nine and a half years in prison, in one man's case. That's what we reached out to, grabbed and held onto. *Personal pride is the most important possession you will ever have.* If you have a sufficient amount, there are no limits in your world. If you don't have it, you may be in rather serious trouble.

When you finish singing, I hope you will understand where we have been, what we did, why it worked for us there, why it would have worked for you too if you had been there, and why and how it applies to everything you do right here in the good old USA. I hope you now understand why I say human potential is nothing more than a state of mind. Most importantly, I hope you can see and understand why I painted the picture you see on the cover of this book. That eagle, with the chain on his leg, represents the difficulties and burdens you will have in life, and there will be many of those. The hope for the future, the real hope for the future, lies in the portion of the painting with the Statue of Liberty and the rays of sunshine. If you can learn to view the world as I do, something good will come out of every day in your life. If you keep faith, you can join me and walk through this world and never have another bad day. Then, and only then, can you escape from the box. Now please sing, "God Bless America!"

God bless America Land that I love
Stand beside her and guide her
Thru the night with a light from above
From the mountains to the prairies
To the oceans white with foam
God bless America my home sweet home
God bless America my home sweet home.

PART TWO

The Price of Success

CONTINUOUS IMPROVEMENT

I hope the previous portion of this book has accomplished two important things: to get your attention and to convince you that there really is a great deal more available to each of us. Now I would like to provide a little "what we can do" now that we are believers.

There is a tremendous ongoing effort in this country to improve the quality of the goods and services produced. One quick look at the state of our economy would lead you to believe the effort has not been particularly successful. An argument could be made that the reason we have not achieved the desired level of success is that we are not even working on the correct problem. We will never be able to improve the quality of the goods and services produced and going out the door until we improve the quality of life of the folks inside who are doing the producing. That is precisely the focus of this book.

The current quality improvement effort is being treated as a scientific effort, with concentration on fixing the processes. Though I intend to dwell on the people and how to help them escape from the box, it is important that we first discuss the more well-known and popular concept, Total Quality Management (TQM) and how it relates to my beliefs. You may have heard of TQM and you also may be a part of a large group of folks in our country who are skeptical about how successful TQM will be.

As I travel around the country, I ask the question, "How many of you sincerely believe that TQM will work?" By far, the majority of the people to whom I speak do not believe TQM will work! However, when I ask the same group of people about my simple idea of developing personal pride in what they do, and just improving things a small amount each day, I find that a large majority of those same people believe my concept will work. It is important to understand that with the exception of a couple of very minor points, there is absolutely no difference between my simple idea of developing personal pride and the TQM concept. I want to explain how these two are nearly identical, but first of all, I need to give you my background on TQM. In November of 1988, I was invited to speak at a conference in Atlanta, Georgia for 1,000 people. Part of those people were military, and the others were defense industry employees who were there to study quality improvement. The man who invited me said, "Would you please come and speak a bit on Total Quality Management?" I said, "Well, you will have to excuse me, I have never heard of that before. You tell me what it is and I guarantee you, I can talk about it."

He sent me a ten-page booklet to read. I read it about ten times and couldn't understand anything it said. It had a lot of technical terms, charts and graphs. I passed it off to my chief engineer and asked him to read it and tell me what it meant. He came back the next day and said, "I can't figure it out either!" I went to Atlanta without a great deal of help. I told the audience that I had been asked to come and speak about Total Quality Management. So, I was going to tell them everything I knew. I told them about the ten-page booklet and that I didn't understand it. I only understood the first three sentences. The first sentence said,

"Survival is our greatest motivator." Based on my personal life experiences I suspect that notion is certainly true. The second sentence said, "Most of the Defense Department and all of the Defense Industry operate in the survival mode every day." I can't prove that, but it wouldn't surprise me. The third sentence said, "Don't worry about a thing, TQM is going to fix all of this." I said, "I'll bet that's bullshit!" I got a standing ovation from those folks. They didn't believe it either and TQM was what they were there to hear about. I left that event assuming I had been clever enough to see right through the latest management fad.

About three months later, I had the privilege of meeting a man at Eglin Air Force Base who spent an hour explaining TQM. That was the first time I had heard it explained. He told me what it was, how it works and what it is supposed to do for the organization. He said there was only one small problem, "We don't know how to get everyone to sign up and participate." I volunteered and said, "I know how to do that. I do it all the time as a hobby." He basically told me to "sit down and shut up," a popular American management style that I will discuss later. The Air Force never accepted my offer.

I would like to share what I know about TQM based on that original lecture and my observations since that time. In my opinion, there are four basic tenets in TQM. The first tenet is the idea of continuous improvement. You know where I stand on that issue. Everything contained in this book, to this point, is dedicated to selling you a belief in continuous improvement.

The first time I ever truly made a bold statement as an amateur speaker was to a tough crowd to whom I suggested that everything we do can be done better. It was at Gunter AFB at the senior NCO (non-commissioned officers) academy. If you want to get hammered in a hurry, go up there and talk to those 200 to 300 senior NCOs and tell them how simple it would be to do their job better. The first thing they do is walk you out of the room and thank you for coming. To the NCOs that day, I made the statement that everything we do can be done better every day. They seriously challenged that, so I offered them the opportunity to prove their point. I asked them to take a piece of paper and list the tasks they perform in the Air Force so well that they could never be improved upon. I received about 200 blank pieces of paper. I have been doing that now for several years and that was the origin of the *Post-it* idea. Nobody has thought of anything yet! The exercise certainly lends immediate perspective. The first basic tenet of TQM is continuous improvement, and nothing proves the validity of that tenet more quickly than a periodic glance at your blank *Post-it*.

LISTEN

The second basic tenet of TQM is the belief that you must listen to the people in the trenches. How well do you think we do that in this country? The basic management style that has been practiced in our nation since long before the day

I was born is, "Sit down, shut up, and do what you are told." We have never listened to the people in the trenches—not in the Air Force, not in the Federal Government, and certainly not in industry. That management style failed and all you have to do to see how badly it failed is to look at any part of our society. When we hire someone we pay for their brain as well as their brawn, but seem unwilling to use the former. If we are ever to recover as a nation, we must listen to the people in the trenches.

A very fine example of this popular management style was illustrated to me several years ago. I had been invited to be the guest speaker at a commanders' conference. Shortly before I left, the secretary for the Air Force general chairing the conference phoned me to finalize my plans. Once travel plans were set, she added, "I have been planning events such as this for more than 20 years. We invite all you theoretically brilliant people to come and speak, but none of us *peons* (her choice of words, so you can tell where she felt she fit in the continuum of importance) are ever invited to hear you speak. How are we supposed to know what is going on in the world?" I simply told her to gather all the peons in a room. I would travel earlier than originally planned, and when I arrived I would speak to the peons first.

When I arrived in Washington, D. C. I was met by this secretary and escorted to an auditorium where she had casually called a meeting for 400 peons. They all showed up! I considered the size of the crowd to be a pretty good measure of their thirst for participation.

Following a one-hour presentation of Human Potential, the first part of this book, we took a coffee break. When they returned I asked, "How many of you have ever heard of TQM?" All 400 people raised their hands. Their boss was a key player in the development of the TQM concept in the Air Force, so naturally they knew it up close and personal. Then I asked how many believed TQM was going to work in the Air Force. Not one hand was raised, which I found rather startling. So, I asked, "What about my simplistic idea of small incremental improvement each day, leading to far greater personal pride?" One hundred percent agreed that would work. I told them perhaps the most important concept they would hear all day was, "TQM and my idea are nearly the same thing! The only difference is I don't call my idea TQM, so it doesn't turn you off."

That night at the commanders' conference I had the privilege of sitting at the head table. Since the head table was a round table, I was provided ample opportunity to speak to the other six gentlemen at the table. The makeup of the group was three two-star generals to my left and three senior executive service civilian employees (three-star general equivalents) to my right. I learned very quickly that night that close proximity to others does not necessarily guarantee good conversation. It seemed I had little in common with the others present at the head table. However, since I was the designated speaker, it appeared in my best interest to establish some rapport with this group, the most influential part of my audience.

Since this was a conference on quality, it seemed appropriate to steer the conversation in that direction. I very casually asked, "How many of you believe TQM is going to work in the Air Force?" My question was met with great enthusiasm, a pumping of arms akin to Jimmy Connors when he won a critical tennis point, and a chorus of six men singing, "Yeah, yeah, yeah!" I pressed on, "Why do you believe that?" They were in total agreement, "Because the four-star general said it will." Since I now had their undivided attention, I decided to pull out all the stops. I asked, "How many of you believe all your people believe TQM will work?" All six repeated the Jimmy Connors act. Now that I had the conversation exactly where I wanted it, I felt it was time to toss them the bait.

I explained to them how ironic it seemed that they were convinced all their people thought TQM was going to work when, in fact, I had asked 400 people on their base that question just a few hours earlier and no one thought TQM would work. My host was very quick to try to provide a logical explanation. He said, "Obviously, it depends on who was in the crowd, what they have been taught, and how clever their leader is." I simply said, "Sir, they all work for you."

My intent was not to embarrass the general, although I am certain I did. My intent was to make what I consider a very critical point. The generals were *not* listening to the people in the trenches. When you don't listen to what the people are saying, you can make decisions based on false assumptions. More often than not, that will result in something less than a desirable outcome.

Perhaps one of the most glaring examples of the type of results you get when you don't listen to the people in the trenches, or when you practice "sit down, shut up and do what you're told" management occurred near the end of my Air Force career. I had traveled most of the way across the United States to pay my last visit to my detachment in New Mexico and tie up all the loose ends. The day was one where I really had to be especially vigilant if I was to going to find one of my little rays of sunshine. I had missed every flight connection and arrived in New Mexico, not at 3:15 p.m. as planned, but at 8:30 p.m. I assumed the billeting office would hold my reservation.

In charge of the billeting office was a young lady probably less than 20 years old, with two stripes. Though I knew by her rank she didn't have much authority, I also knew how important she was in my life at that precise moment. She was going to provide me a room.

I walked up to her and said, "Hi, I'm Colonel Hubbard and I have a reservation." She responded, "Yes sir, I have your reservation right here, but unfortunately I can't give you a room." I suggested that having a reservation in their establishment did not appear to be of much value and proceeded to ask several questions. Then I realized there was one obvious question I had not asked, "Are there any empty rooms?" Without even blinking she answered that question, "Yes, sir, but I'm afraid I can't give you one." Then came the part I had been waiting for, the standard American answer anytime things are not working well. "It is not my fault!" She explained to me that it was the computer's fault. She even persisted and went so far as to show me on her computer why I could not have a room, even after I told her I didn't care to discuss the subject with her computer. Then I said I would like to speak to her boss, whom she had been referring to as "him." The *him* was a colonel, the Base Commander. So, I said, "I want to talk to *him*." This young lady, who was becoming more embarrassed by the moment, took a deep breath and said, "I'm sorry, sir, you can't talk to him. He is at a formal party and cannot be disturbed."

She was wrong! I called the command post and requested the Base Commander's presence immediately at the billeting office. They must have assumed from the tone of my voice that this was an emergency because the colonel walked in about three minutes later. After I explained the circumstances, he asked the same questions I had asked and he got the same answers. When he asked about empty rooms and she said yes, he quietly said, "Give Colonel Hubbard an empty room."

At that point the Base Commander turned to me and said something I will never forget. His words were, "Don't be upset with her; she did exactly what I told her to do. Use the new computer system. Make it work. If it doesn't work or if anyone gives you a hard time, call me and I will take care of the problem."

I could no longer control the rage that had been building in me for the past 45 minutes. I blurted out, "You know what I'll bet? You are the busiest colonel on the base and you are the dumbest colonel I ever met. You told this young lady and probably hundreds of others in your command, 'Don't think. Sit down, shut up, and do what you are told.'"

Sad, but true, this popular management style permeates our nation. Until we change, until we listen to the people in the trenches, until we allow them to think—or better yet, demand that they think—we are destined to continue down the wrong road.

ACCOUNTABILITY

There are actually two separate and distinct parts to the third basic tenet, as I understand it. This tenet contends that we are all basically good people and that we would all like to do better. But we can't because *we are all maxed out.* Even if we weren't, we would be unable to progress because processes as TQM names them, or the systems, as I call them, are all so screwed up we can make no progress.

Let's take on the first part: We are all maxed out. I hope, if I have accomplished nothing else in this book up to this point, that I have convinced you none of us is maxed out. In fact, none of us has even scratched the surface. So I completely discount this part of the third tenet.

The second part of this tenet holds that the processes (systems) are so screwed up we can't make any progress. Apparently, some people believe that there is a mysterious process making things happen. I believe there is just one process/system that makes things happen: humans. When humans act, things happen. If humans do not act, nothing happens.

When you are at work, look around the room. You and the other people there with you are the system. Not the machines, not the computers, not the buildings; the people make up the system. If the system is broken it is the fault of the people. If the system is ever going to be fixed, it must be fixed by the people. People, and only people can make the system work better. If George Bush had understood that, he might still be president. He wasn't even convinced that there was a problem with the system. After the majority of citizens recognized we had an economic crisis, and Mr. Bush finally admitted the system was in some trouble, unfortunately, he then said, "It is not my fault. It's the fault of the Japanese." Once we can no longer hide from the truth, we place the blame elsewhere.

George Bush fell into the same trap with many other Americans. We hate to admit what we are responsible for is what is broken, so we hide in denial for as long as possible. I call that the Richard Nixon syndrome. Now all Americans must step up to our responsibilities. We built the existing system. We broke the existing system. It is no one's fault but ours and we are the only ones who can fix the system. The bottom line is that the system is broken. It is immaterial who broke the system or how; what is critical is that we recognize we can and must fix it, and soon.

CULTURAL CHANGE

That brings us to the difficult part, what must we do. The TQM gurus will tell us that we must create a total cultural change, the fourth basic tenet. There are about as many definitions of total cultural change as there are people espousing the need. Regardless of the definition there is one area of agreement among all the advocates and that is that this change will take five to seven years. I often wonder if it takes that long simply because that is how long we must pay the TQM consultants.

Don't misunderstand me. I agree there is a desperate need for the cultural change. However, I do not believe it should take five to seven years. I believe we can have significant results in five to seven months, when the leaders of an organization are truly committed. Late one afternoon, I spoke to an Air Force group of 430 people. I suggested if they really wanted to get the ball rolling they would all have to accept some responsibility and take action. I asked them to provide one signed quality improvement idea to their commander. I wanted solutions. When we left, the boss was very skeptical about the outcome. By noon the next day, he had 430 solutions. Unfortunately, he wasn't committed and there was no follow-up.

What is my basic definition of this new culture? It is a new way of life. A life where we each play a vital role and every individual is accountable for his or her actions. A world where anonymous tips have no place, and where there is great trust and respect. Above all, there is tremendous pride in the way we do our business. It is an organization, or family, where people are willing to stand in line for a long time just for the privilege of being associated with us. We do our very best every day, knowing full well we must come back and do even better tomorrow. But the big question is still unanswered. How do we get there?

Several years ago I attended a Fourth Annual TQM Conference at an organization which employs about 25,000 people. The head of the organization spent the opening hour providing an historical perspective on their progress over the previous four years. When he was on his last slide–one covered with numbers–a young man in the front row stood up and asked, "Sir, can you point to the specific progress we made this last year?" The boss simply pointed at one of the numbers and said, "Yes, this past year we have trained 3,217 people." The man obviously wasn't impressed because he retorted, "That is not our job! Where are the production results?"

The boss very calmly stepped over to the podium and pointed out, "Don't forget, this is TQM–it takes a major cultural change and it will take five to seven years. This is only our fourth year."

This specific example should give anyone cause for alarm because the organization was a federal agency. They had spent millions of dollars on training in four years. They had achieved virtually no measurable results, but they were not concerned because they knew it would take five to seven years to get results. Unless we have unlimited funds and five to seven years during which no significant progress is required, I suggest that there must be a better answer.

The answer may not be infinite training. One item we can agree on is the need for change.

ATTITUDE, AGAIN

At a large corporate quality conference, I once had the privilege of listening as 350 corporate production and manufacturing vice presidents discussed what to change. Considerable discussion narrowed the field to attitudes or behavior. Further discussion lead to consensus. Attitudes are something people are born with that can't readily be changed. Behavior modification is something we can work with. Once the consensus was reached everyone went to lunch.

By a stroke of misfortune, I was the first speaker after lunch. I started the vice presidents' afternoon off right by telling them I felt their decision before lunch was wrong. Changing behavior to create this required culture change was analogous to putting a very small bandaid on a gaping wound. It probably would not do any good, but not to worry, it probably would not last very long either.

One example of why I believe as I do comes from the prisons in North Vietnam. With a large club or a rubber hose, or a set of ropes, the Vietnamese could change our behavior anytime they wanted. However, they could not change our attitude. Therefore, if they wanted us to do something again, a few days later, they had to come back and change our behavior again. If you want truly lasting changes, you must change people's attitudes.

Possibly another more relevant example would make the point even better. On the night of November 9, 1989, I was watching the six o'clock news in my room in a crummy yet very historical hotel. I was waiting to go to a dinner after which I was to speak. As I watched the news I suddenly realized I had very large tears running down my cheeks. I was watching people climbing over the Berlin wall and becoming free. I was totally submerged in the same emotion I felt on March 4, 1973 as I left Hanoi. I was observing 100 million people becoming free. Their behavior had been changed for over 50 years by communism, but their attitude had never changed. They wanted to be free, just like you and me.

I hope I can convince you that you cannot change people's behavior and make that a permanent fix. You can only make a permanent fix if you change people's attitude, the way they view the world, and what they are willing to do. But, you cannot force a change in attitude. People who think you can force attitude changes are the same people who think you can mandate quality. I want to tell you a little story that will help you understand the absurdity of that idea.

Early on in my speaking career, the Air Force videotaped one of my speeches. Since several attendees had asked for a tape, I asked the Air Force for it. You guessed it, the answer was no. I said, "It is my speech." To which they replied, "It is our tape!" I asked what they would think if I refused to make any more speeches. They suggested that they would order me to speak. I pointed out to them if they were dumb enough to order me to speak, no doubt they were also dumb enough to order me to be sincere! You cannot force attitude changes. Attitude changes come by giving people guidance, by helping them see the advantages of doing things better, quicker and smarter. People especially need to see how a change in their attitude will benefit them personally. People only participate of their own free will. So, you have to change their attitude in order to motivate them to participate. That's why I do what I do. TQM, or some variation, is a requirement for our future. Instead of fighting it, we need to participate in it. TQM is not a program with a start and finish. TQM must become a way of life. Attitudes and perceptions are critical because, in essence, they rule the world. All decisions, good or bad, are made based on attitudes and perceptions. Ordinarily, a bad decision results from bad perception, even at the presidential level. In fact in recent years that seems to have become almost fashionable.

In 1983, President Reagan reviewed the bidding for the previous year, and found that we spent several billion dollars a year on workmen's compensation for civilian Government employees who are injured on the job. He decided that needed attention. In an attempt to fix the problem, he called in his experts, the National Safety Council, and asked them for a recommendation. They said, "We have a standard in the National Safety Council that a three percent reduction in mishaps in a year's time is a very fine accomplishment. Very few organizations can achieve that."

The President accepted that as a suitable goal. So he put the word out that every Government agency, worldwide, would reduce civilian on-the-job injuries by three percent per year over the next five years. You know what happens when the President says something like that? Directives flow through all the layers of bureaucracy, and eventually arrive on the desk of the poor person charged with implementation–guys like me, the Chief of Safety. I actually received a clear text message from my headquarters outlining the President's pro rata share for my organization. The directive said "Your goal for 1984 at Eglin AFB is to injure 118 people and kill two." The President didn't make a mistake by trying to solve the problem. His mistake was in allowing the bureaucracy to distort his direction. Well, I didn't think that was a particularly positive direction, so I merely drafted a little message and sent it right back to them and said, "Please send me two volunteers! Nobody wants to die down here!"

At this point it is critical to understand the part attitude plays. If my people's attitude had been based on what they heard most of their lives, "sit down, shut up and do what you're told," they would have become part of the problem and participated in the potential disaster. They knew better. But, since their attitude was "we are smarter than that," they become part of the solution. The outcome of our effort is explained in the "enthusiasm" section of this book.

I think it important for you to understand where I come from. I spend my whole life racing around trying to change attitudes and helping people become part of the solution. I have had reasonable success, but almost everywhere I go people ask, "Would you mind sitting down so the rest of us can take a break?" I have been told repeatedly that nobody can change the world by themselves. I will not accept that. I am still trying. I believe if I can do this long enough, maybe I can change the world! We need to understand how important one person's personality or one person's attitude can be to the crowd.

Back in 1988, I was going to Cannon AFB. I don't know if you have ever been to Cannon, but to get there you fly to Lubbock, Texas, and then drive northwest until you fall off the earth and you are at Cannon. I was going to be there for three days. I had no clue how I was going to kill some spare time I would have during my three days at Cannon. As I have gone around speaking, people have told me, that "if you want to do this professionally, you have to read the books by all the big guys because they will tell you what you're supposed to say." You have probably heard of Zig Ziglar, the world-famous motivational speaker. I bought one of his books, *Top Performance*, at the airport on the way to Cannon. During my spare time while there, I read it.

Mr. Ziglar tells an interesting story about a week he had spent in Kansas City, where I grew up. He had been speaking all week and on Friday afternoon he was on his way home to Dallas. Like all of us who travel regularly, he arrived late at the airport and stood at the end of a line. That particular day, Zig arrived at the airport and there was a long line and he was all the way in the back. It looked like he was probably going to miss his flight. He noticed the ticket agent at the next counter getting ready to open and there was no line. When she opened, Zig dashed up and when he got to the counter, the ticket agent looked up at him and said, "The three o'clock flight to Dallas has been cancelled." Ever happen to you? Happens to me all the time. I always bang on the desk, call them dirty names and demand my money back. After I get through screaming and shouting, the flight is still cancelled. My behavior doesn't change anything.

Ziglar had already been through that, obviously, and when the ticket agent said the flight had been cancelled, he said, "Fantastic!" She looked at him like he was out of his mind, the sort of a look that says, "What's your problem, Fella?" And he said, "Ma'am, there are only three reasons why anybody would cancel a flight to Dallas, Texas. Number one, something must be wrong with that airplane; number two, something must be wrong with the person who is going to fly that airplane; number three, something must be wrong with the weather they're going to fly that airplane in. Now ma'am, if any one of those three situations exists, I don't want to be up there. I want to be right down here! Fantastic!" Interesting thought! A positive view of what you and I always see as a bad situation. One hundred people waiting for the airplane were now listening for whatever surprise was coming next. The flight to Dallas wasn't really cancelled, it was merely delayed for three hours. Besides, Zig told the ticket agent that he was pleased to find himself in an excellent facility–a warm, comfortable, modern and free building–for the duration and planned to make good use of the next three hours. Ziglar was convinced that he received a good deal that day and I suspect that fellow passengers overhearing his exchange with the ticket agent shared his feeling.

That's what one person's attitude can do. Every person has the opportunity to influence the lives of many other people every day. You can add to what they already perceive as their overburden, or you can become that ray of sunshine they need. If you plant the positive seed, everybody around you will grab onto it and run with it. Please, go out and plant some positive seeds. Another story represents the other side of the coin. I boarded a plane in Atlanta about 6:00 a.m. one Saturday following a Friday night red eye flight from Seattle. Do you know the lovely flight attendant who is always there to greet you with a smile? Well, she was there minus the smile. So I thought I would help her a bit. With my biggest smile, I said, "Good Morning! How are you today?" Her very curt answer was "I am here!" All I could respond was, "I'm glad you're not flying the plane!" We all meet people every day. We have an opportunity to influence their lives and attitudes, for better or worse. The choice is ours.

Another subject Ziglar mentions in his book is the subject of choices. He warns, not to let others "cancel your day." I relate those words to one of my favorite sayings, which is, "You can't do that." When a boss says that to you, what the boss really means is that *he* or *she* is not willing to try. Do not let anyone tell you what *you* can or cannot do. People don't know how clever you are and they certainly don't know how hard you are willing to work. The next time somebody says "no," just say, "Thank you! You have just provided me with my next goal to work on."

During the year 1976 I really had three bosses. None was positive, but none as negative as my immediate supervisor. My first day on the job he called me in to see why I had volunteered for what he called "the worst job in the Air Force." I had just become chief of scheduling for a tactical fighter wing and my new boss was showing me a scheduling form, a big piece of paper with little squares all over it to record the tail number of the airplane, the pilot, the weapons officer, the bomb load, the bullet load, gas load and the route and range–just millions of little pieces of information. My supervisor computed that if I filled this form out properly every day over the next year, I would fill in seventeen million little squares. That's square filling at its very best. He said, "Remember, you are expected to fill in all the squares correctly every time." It's like starting the baseball season batting one thousand. There's nowhere to go but down. He made a bad assumption. He assumed what they had been doing was the best they could do. I didn't assume that, or I wouldn't have taken the job.

For the year I worked for him, I kept a book and listed everything he told me I couldn't do. I dated the item and recorded the time. Then I left a blank line to fill in when I completed the project. When completed, I noted the date. I left at the end of a year and gave him the book which was full and said, "Here's a book I wrote while I was working for you; you ought to read it some day." About 90 percent of the tasks my boss assumed couldn't be done were done the same day. In the section entitled "innovation" I will explain how you fill seventeen million squares–creatively!

This book was written to try to change your attitude. It's not to change your attitude for a few minutes or a few days. My desire is to change your attitude for the rest of your life so you can be a participant in all the things that need to happen. I call this section, "The Price of Success." I have chosen that name for a reason. Far too many people assume that the price of success is too high a price to pay. I want to convince you that the price is not only not too high, it is in fact *free*! I am going to discuss the qualities you were born with, but may not yet have fully developed.

Price, *P R I C E*, was chosen so I can remember what I'm supposed to talk about during my speeches. *P* stands for *pride,* *R* stands for *responsibility,* *I* stands for *innovation,* *C* stands for *courage* and *E* stands for *enthusiasm.* I will explain how these qualities fit in your life and how with these five qualities fully developed, you can conquer the world no matter where you started or where you think you want to finish. I believe after reading the first section you have an idea of where I place pride.

PRIDE

Pride is the cornerstone of everything we will ever do in this world. Pride is the most important, number one quality in your life. Not pride as in egotist, but pride that I call real pride. Real pride occurs when you do the right thing every time, no matter what others say or think. I believe my best example is our interrogations in North Vietnam. The interrogator would come by on a regular basis and ask, "Wouldn't you like to sign this little thing (and betray your country)? Nobody will ever know you did it and if you don't, we'll probably hurt you." Neither one was a good option. We always attempted the right thing, refused and we took our lumps. Not because we would be praised for what we did, because no one would ever know what we did there, but because *we* knew it was the right thing to do and it's what we got paid to do and we knew we did it better than anyone else on Earth. It created a level of pride deep inside each of us that forced us to go out each day and do our very best only for ourselves.

A management concept around for a lot of years says you have to go by every one of your employees, pat them on the head and praise them. This is called "stroking." Most management textbooks and psychology books warn that if you don't stroke your folks, they may not perform well. I don't do stroking very well because I don't have much confidence in the concept. The flaw in this concept is that if you miss stroking for a day, folks might quit performing for a day. We have created a society where everyone demands instant rewards, a society where people have to be pampered and coddled in order to get them to do what they ought to do anyway. Real pride is why people perform, not for rewards, but because it makes them feel so good, to the extent that they don't even care what other people think. They perform at that level because they know they do it better than anyone else, possibly including their boss. When you arrive at this level of understanding, your job becomes a very simple task. You love what you do and you are very,

very proud of the outcome. You would do it whether or not you received any praise. Real pride starts with you. I believe this is the cultural change discussed in TQM.

An article appeared in the paper several years ago that described the educational difference between American and Asian students. It was a super article because it pointed out a different way of thinking which is also what cultural change means. The article stated that American families assume it takes 90 percent talent and 10 percent effort to accomplish a given task. Asian people believe just the opposite. They believe it takes 10 percent talent and 90 percent effort. I swear it takes 1 percent talent and 99 percent effort. It's what you believe you can do coupled with the amount of energy you are willing to expend. And, Asian students are surpassing the Americans by leaps and bounds! Although they make up only 3 percent of the population in the United States, 46 percent of the students at Harvard and M.I.T. are Asian. Asians view the world very differently than we do. It would help us greatly if we would consider their world view.

RESPONSIBILITY

Being proud is very important. There is another part of our world that worries me a great deal. That is the inability of the American people, as a general rule, to accept responsibility for the outcome of the things for which they are responsible. That really is a tough one. You have to make decisions every day. It's like driving down the road at 100 miles an hour and you come to a fork that goes left and right. You have to make that decision instantly. Or, you can go straight ahead and crash and burn. If your desire is to survive, then you have to learn to make decisions.

The reasons most of us are so reluctant to do that is, first of all, we may feel at times like we're not clever enough or smart enough and don't have enough knowledge to make those decisions. Sometimes we have the knowledge and simply don't have the confidence to make good decisions. We don't know what the outcome is going to be, which creates some level of risk, so we would rather pass. The reason most people won't make decisions is because of the tremendous amount of stress associated with making a decision when there is no guarantee of how it is going to turn out. The last section of this part of the book has a short stress-awareness/reducing exercise.

Have you ever muttered under your breath, "If I was in charge for one day, I would change all of this!" You *are* in charge. Decide to accept responsibility for whatever you are in charge of no matter where you are in the system or how small your part. You are in charge of your piece of the world. Your piece is your responsibility and you probably know more about that piece than anyone. Your responsibility is to fix it when it's broken and when it isn't broken, to make it run better, to improve it. Some way, some how, I don't care how you do it, but find a way to improve your piece of the world. The system has allowed us for years to blame lack of progress on the TQM tenet which I described earlier which says that we're all maxed out. The system won't let you perform and excel. That's untrue; the system *will* allow excellence. You must not wait to hear it is okay to act. Demand your right and accept your responsibility to act.

If you work for me and you see that something is broken, you better fix it. I never did internal self-inspections in my organization because I expected all my people to act when they saw situations requiring action. They did that. While in the Air Force, when the I.G. (Inspector General) showed up, he always said, "Tell me about your internal inspection program." I told him I didn't have one. I did not believe in it. I never have. Make it right as soon as you discover it's broken, press on and it's business as usual every day. We were constantly improving. The I.G. phoned me once to warn me he was coming soon, and told me that I needed to start getting ready. I told him, "I have been ready for the past ten years. Come on over!" I sincerely believed that. If you work at that level all the time and accept that kind of responsibility, you're always ready for inspection. If you are responsible for a tiny piece of the puzzle which needs fixing, and you know how, do it!

If you can't fix it because you feel your solution exceeds your authority, at least do your boss a favor and let the boss know something is broken. Since your boss already has plenty of problems to solve, don't send the boss another problem, send a problem with several viable solutions. Send a little note: "This is broken, these are the options available, what I would suggest is....." After your boss reads your note, he or she has a responsibility to respond. Your boss either has to select one of your solutions, or be prepared to explain to you why your solution is not viable. If unable to implement a solution, your boss can only pass your information up the chain of command. It can only be passed to the top level of management who then must fix it. If that person is not prepared to fix it, then he or she has to be prepared to find another job. Each of us must step up to the fact that we are not at maximum capacity. Each one of us must make a decision and be prepared to accept the responsibility.

The higher you climb up the ladder of authority, the greater the level of responsibility becomes. Perhaps the most critical responsibility of the leader of any organization is to create a vision, a sense of where the organization is going. Not just any vision, but a brilliant vision. At the conclusion of this book I will discuss a corporation where I spoke, a corporation whose vision was to achieve the industry standard. They had done that. Unfortunately the industry standard only required them to produce 41 percent of their products successfully. I told them, "Where I come from we do not strive to achieve industry standard, we set the standard, and we certainly would never set the standard at 41 percent!"

Shortly after, I spoke at a corporate quality conference where they demanded a much higher standard. They required their suppliers to provide 94 percent of products delivered on time and 94 percent were required to work the first time used, without repair. Of course, that left the door open for six percent of their patients to die in the operating room. But, at least they had a higher standard.

Another call requested my support in a new effort to move a company from number 22 to number 20, worldwide in gross business. Initially I declined simply because I didn't want to be on a team that only wanted to be number 20. I suggested to the corporate president that a better vision would be number one! When he asked how I expected to achieve such results, I offered him the following formula. Produce everything on or before delivery date. Ensure 100 percent of your products work. And, sell your products at a price below everyone else's. He insisted his employees would not sign up to try such a bold endeavor. I told him if he was willing to stand in front of his employees and tell them this was his vision, I would go along and provide the atmosphere. At the first gathering there were approximately 1,000 employees. When the president explained his vision there was shock on the faces of the employees and a reasonable amount of snickering. The first thing I did when it was my turn to speak was to attempt to establish some ground rules. I asked, "Will all of you in this audience who were hired to do things wrong please stand . . . and then leave . . . we will no longer need your services!" Need I say more?

You see, the leader must do more than just create a vision. The leader must also sell it to all the players; the players must buy on a non-returnable basis. It must become a shared vision if there is to be any hope of success. Then comes the real hard part. The leader must create the atmosphere where great things are going to happen everyday, where everyone believes they have a great future, and where everyone believes the leader sincerely cares about their contributions to the vision and about their individual futures.

A corporate president asked me a question following a speech one time that I had never been asked before. He said, "I believe I understood your message very well and feel reasonably comfortable about being able to apply it to my employees. My concern is how can I apply this to my 14-year old son?" I replied, "The same way you will with your employees. Make sure you demonstrate a sincere interest in the outcome and their future. Without the sincere interest, you will fail."

INNOVATION

If you are going to improve your piece of the system and do it well, innovation is the key. It's how change comes about. Contrary to widespread belief, taking the hard way is not required. We need innovation and creativity. For some mysterious reason, some of us believe that innovation is not part of our job. Lots of folks seem to believe that innovation is reserved for a select few who are in charge of new ideas. Those same folks don't see themselves as creative, so let's see how simple innovation can be.

For a clearer focus on innovation let's go back to 1987. On the night before I went to Charleston to speak, (where I forgot my pants) one of my listeners came up to me and told me, "You know, you're a boring speaker!" I said, "Thank you very much!" He said, "You don't tell any jokes." I said, "I'm not a comedian. Do I look like a comedian to you?" He said, "Well, you ought to tell some jokes. It would be easier to handle." So, following my own message of improving every day, I took his advice. I stopped in the Atlanta Airport the next day to get a *Reader's Digest*. I was going to find a joke to use that night. When I got to Charleston, I found I had forgotten my pants. That was a lot funnier than the joke I found but never used. But, I believe it to be a very appropriate story that has something to do with innovation.

Another example of innovation is a story about two young coeds, who were traveling from the northeast along the east coast to Fort Lauderdale for their spring break. In South Carolina, they were going about 120 miles per hour and a sheriff stopped them. The sheriff came up to the car and said, "All right, Ma'am, let's see your driver's license." The driver handed him her license, sat there for a few seconds, then she reached into her purse, pulled out a second card and handed it to the sheriff. He stood there, looked at the card for a minute, then he got a big grin on his face, and he said, "OK, OK! You know, if you drive like this for very long you are going to get hurt and I'd just as soon you didn't get hurt in South Carolina. If you promise to behave yourself, and slow down, I'll turn you loose." So he turned them loose with no ticket. She started on down the road and her friend turned to her and said, "I give-up. How did you do that? What was the second card you gave the sheriff?" "Oh, it's very simple, that's one of the cards from my Monopoly game. That's the *get out of jail free* card!"

What is innovation all about? If you don't like the results you are getting, invent a better, smarter, simpler way. That's really all there is to it. I went to a training session in California when I became Chief of Safety. I had no clue as to what I was supposed to do, so the Air Force sent me to this California school for two weeks. The first week they read me all the safety regulations. I have never seen them since and I hope I never do. The second week there was a management seminar which was very good. The speaker had some neat techniques for self-discovery. One of his techniques that I thought was quite ingenious was a question to the 32 people in the room, all of whom were lieutenant colonels or colonels. "Do you guys have any idea what you get paid to do?" Of course, we all knew. He asked us to give him the answer in three words or less and he wrote our responses on the board.

When he finished he said, "Do you know why I love to come and speak to Air Force officers? Because you are all so stupid! Nobody in this room knows what they are getting paid to do!" He explained that each of us is like a finger-print. "Everybody is slightly different, everybody is unique based on their background, environment, education and so on. Whatever that unique capability is, which each one of you owns, you still get paid for the same thing. You get paid to make the organization better the day you depart than it was the day you arrived. That is the sum total for which you are paid." I have used that concept in some ways.

You are probably familiar with performance appraisal systems. The one we used in the Federal Government for civil servants was probably one of the most worthless things anybody ever invented. The Government civilian appraisal system has four categories: outstanding, excellent, fully successful or you don't belong here. The system measures people's ability based on how many mistakes they make. I have never done anything in life where we measured against a negative standard. Using this system, you have to find out what a person is in charge of, and then tell them they can make a specific number of mistakes. In my former organization, one of the mandatory statements in the job description concerns security. What do you put in there? You can make two security errors a year? No way! Not if you work for me! So when people came to work for me, I explained what the rules were. If you come to work for me, and get there on time every day, and do every single thing you are told to do, and do it perfectly, you are fully successful. I guarantee, that will get everybody's attention, including the union. That's how I feel about it. Some people have told me, "That's no good! You leave no room to improve." In response, I simply told them there is room for improvement, when you operate independently. You know what is required, and you do not need to be told to do those things. You can work your way up to excellent by doing those things.

The way you move up to the outstanding category, where everybody wants to be, is to come up with a new way to do the things you are presently doing so that the system works better. That's what innovation is and that's what we get paid to do. If you wanted to get an "outstanding" in my organization at the end of the appraisal period, you just wrote down the rating you thought you deserved and then listed all the things that you had invented that made the system work better. If you had no list, odds are you were not outstanding. What we are looking for is a way to encourage people to try to change things to make them better and there are a lot of changes required. Everything we do could be done a lot better. I can't think of all those things, your boss can't think of all those things, he or she can't even see all those things. You must play your role in making those little changes. If we all performed at this level, the Government wouldn't have to spend $100 million for TQM! We have been getting paid to do this all along. We just haven't done it and it's time to start doing it.

Now for the payoff, let's go back to when I was the chief of scheduling and had to fill seventeen million squares annually. It required creativity. But, I was brand new to the fighter business and didn't know what I was supposed to do. There was one thing that appalled me. There were 48 airplanes sitting on the ramp which represented $350 million worth of resources. Out of those 48 airplanes, we were able to launch 36 sorties per day. I thought that sounded inefficient. We should be doing better than that. When I talked with the air crews they said, "We'd fly more if we had more planes. The maintenance crews never give us enough planes." The standard American answer is to always blame poor performance elsewhere. Even the "leaders" of our country, the President and Congress, do that every day!

I crossed the street and talked with the maintenance guys and with a chief master sergeant who was the chief of maintenance scheduling. I asked him, "Chief, would you explain to me how the system works?" He took the book out and showed me that you get this many airplanes on the ramp and there is a certain percent you get to fly and the rest are down for some kind of scheduled or nonscheduled maintenance. Basically, out of the 48 airplanes, I received 26 every day to fly. Out of those, by regulation, 6 had to be held aside for spares, so only 20 could fly every day. I then asked him, "If I send all the planes to fly, and they come back and I want to send them out again, how many do I know I can send back out?" He said, "That's easy! 66 percent." I asked him where he got that figure. He told me it was written in the regs. "How many can I fly if I want to send them back out a third time?" His response was 33 percent of the original 20. He said that was in the regs, too.

I asked to read the regs. After I finished reading, I told him there were only a few words he left out. The reg actually says, "As a minimum, you have to turn 66 percent of the first launch the second time and 33 percent the third time." The chief said, "That's the way we have always done it!" I told him I didn't doubt that. Then I asked him a simple math problem: "If I launch four aircraft, which go out, drop bombs, and come back, and I want to send them out again, how many can I consistently launch the second time?" He said, "You can always get three out of the four." "When they come back, how many can I launch the next time?" "You can always get two out of three." "That's 75 percent and 50 percent, not 66 percent and 33 percent. Maybe that sounds insignificant, but that equates to nine more sorties per day, or a 25 percent increase in productivity! Tomorrow let's try that." He said, "I can't do that. My boss won't let me." I said, "Don't ask your boss. Let's just do it and see what happens. You and I are making the schedule. Nobody will ever know it until it's over!" So we did it!

The next day we launched 45 sorties instead of 36. We launched a 25 percent increase in productivity. We didn't spend a dime. We simply used all the resources already available! One of the things a guy on the flight line will tell you is that the more you fly those aircraft, the better they perform. Before long, we quit using six spares. Before long, we rarely needed any. About a week after we started I went over to see the chief again, and I said, "Chief, I have a new proposition for you. (He always liked to see me coming.) I have six airplanes parked out there on the ramp that don't do anything. Give me four of those and let me put them in the first launch and let's watch and see what happens. Don't worry about spares. If they break, they break." We took those four aircraft and put them in the system, and the next day we launched 54 sorties. Now we are looking at a 50 percent increase in productivity of a $350 million resource. It took eight days and it didn't cost us anything. We went from the lowest sortie generation rate in what was the Tactical Air Command (TAC) to the highest in just eight days, and it was free!

Now let me tell you what happens when you do that. In TAC at the time, we were flying so many aircraft we didn't know what to do. The command inspector general sent a team down to investigate us. Obviously, we were cheating! They sent a lieutenant colonel down to check on me. I gave him a clip board with paper and pencil and told him to go down to the end of the runway, and every time an airplane took off with my name on the tail, to put a hash mark down. At that time, the identifier painted on the tail of our planes was ED. Everybody in town thought I owned all the airplanes. The lieutenant colonel recorded the launches every day for a week. We launched 54 sorties a day. We were really maxing the system out. We were directed to cut back. The way we cut back was to stand down and fly no sorties on Fridays, instead of reducing by a few sorties per day.

The stand down day, Friday, allowed another possibility for improvement. The way it usually works is that the guys with college educations go out and fly very expensive jets all day and then bring them back at night for the maintenance crews to fix. If maintenance can't get them fixed in the dark, then they get to work on the weekends. We started something new! We gave maintenance the whole fleet on Friday morning and they had all day to work on all the airplanes. A lot of interesting things came out of that arrangement. The first thing that happened was that we went from a nominal 55 percent "in commission" rate on Monday morning to 95 percent on Friday night! This was a first in the history of the Air Force: the TAC maintenance crews did not have to work on the weekends. Second, we sustained a 25 percent increase in sortie rate with no one having to work weekends for a year. That's what innovation is all about. It was not harder, it was simpler. It was cheaper, it was better. Everybody made out on the deal. Innovation opportunities are available to each one of us every day. You may not own a fleet of jets but the basic principle applies to any resource.

COURAGE

When you identify an opportunity for innovation, you need the courage to approach your boss. As a major and the chief of scheduling, it took no courage on my part to tell that chief master sergeant to defy his boss. It did take a lot of courage on the chief's part to press on without approval, even though he knew the plan was better. Courage is the basis for confidence. Courage is the result of launching into new ventures repeatedly, and recognizing that periodically you will fall flat on your face and you will probably get hurt. *That is not failure.* Failure sets in when you don't get up and try again. There is a famous quote which says, "Navigators are never lost, they are only temporarily disoriented." I have a corollary to that which says, "There is no failure. There is only temporary setback." The only way in life that you can fail is if you don't try.

It takes courage to push a new idea up from the bottom. However, I would contend that it takes equal, if not greater, courage on the part of a supervisor to let that subordinate try, knowing full well that the subordinate will make some mistakes. There is nothing wrong with making a few mistakes, as long as you learn from them and don't repeat them. That is how leaders achieve their level of success–always trying, sometimes stumbling, a few falls along the way, always learning, and never quitting.

The leaders of our nation, our industry and our education system must learn and employ a new style of leadership. It will be a critical part of the cultural change. It will be a style where stumbling and falling will not be condemned as failure and where leaders no longer step on the hand of the worker who has fallen, but take the fallen worker's hand and help the worker up, and discuss the shortcoming to insure it won't be repeated. It will take courage on the part of every person in the system, but with that style of leadership, we can become a team, and it is free!

For several years, I had a man work for me as one of my directors. He used to come to me routinely and say, "I need three more people to do my job." I finally tired of hearing that so I had him sit down one day and I took a piece of paper and wrote down the names of his staff. Then I rank ordered them all from top to bottom by performance. I looked at each one and scored their performance against the desired 100 percent. If you remember, I used this same method back on the first few pages of this book to show how I could reduce my Air Force budget by approximately one million dollars each year. Now I also used it to help people increase their courage and desire to do better. When I felt I had convinced my director that he really was 3.3 employees short, I also told him, "You are not going to believe this, but I am not going to give you any more resources until you learn to use the ones you already have.

Once you have all these people working close to 100% come see me and we will see how many you need then."

A short time later, one of the people I had rated at 30 percent had retired. Nobody missed a beat. Everything was still getting done. The next year we lost another person. Nobody missed either of them. Nobody knew they were gone and I did not fill those positions. I had a strange way of doing business. I didn't fill positions just because they were there, I filled them when I felt we needed them. I was saving those two positions for something else. I knew some day, somebody would come along and say I had to eliminate two positions and I could say, "There you are. Take those two where nobody lives." That's the way you have to do business. Being the boss is not always a fun deal. But you have to be realistic. We came here to do the job. Nobody ever said the job would be easy.

ENTHUSIASM

If you are proud, ready to step up to your responsibilities, innovative, and possess great courage . . . you will be seriously successful because so few with whom you will compete are nurturing those traits. But, let us assume you (and your family or organization) are already achieving at high levels and you still desire to climb higher . . . you only need one other thing . . . enthusiasm. All the people you have ever known or heard about, who were truly successful possessed enormous enthusiasm for what they were doing. They were passionately committed to their cause.

One of the greatest attributes of enthusiasm is that it is contagious. Almost like a disease, inserted at any point in the system, it will multiply and spread until it affects the entire system. If you are the leader and desire to accomplish great things, then by golly, you had best be very enthusiastic. But, more importantly, if you are the leader and expect, or need others to accomplish those great things you had better be able to create that level of enthusiasm in others.

Here are a couple of examples of what enthusiasm can do for you and your organization and why it is so important. Ten years ago, my next door neighbor was a young man who had been a staff sergeant in the Air Force. He had been in para-rescue. He had been at a party where people had been smoking dope and he became guilty by association. No one witnessed him smoking dope but the assumption was made that he did. His squadron commander called him in and said, "You are about ready to re-enlist. If you try to re-enlist, I will court-martial you. If you go quietly I'll forget anything ever happened." That scared him and he left the Air Force.

A year later when I saw him, he was holding down five jobs. He was working from about 3:00 a.m. to midnight. He finished high school, but set no records, even though he had a tremendous amount of drive. I sat down and talked with him and asked him why he didn't get back into the Air Force. He said he had tried but the Air Force wouldn't have him. Every time he went down to the recruiting office, the recruiter told him, "Everybody in this town knows you. You can't get in here. You are the bad guy." So I made this young man a deal, "You do exactly what I tell you and go out there and make something of your life, and I'll get you back in the Air Force." We had an agreement.

Later, I took him with me to a speaking engagement. When I finished my speech, we went downtown to the local recruiters. I got him in the Air Force just like that. Their screening system was zero. As soon as he got back in, he went back to para-rescue school and became requalified. He went to Holloman AFB and during the next three years—at night, during the weekends, on his lunch hour, and during his spare time—he went to college. He finished a four- year college degree in three years! He did this in his spare time and carried a 4.0 grade average.

On a beautiful day in June of the next year, I had the privilege of going to San Antonio to witness him receive his gold bars. He is now a captain in the Air Force. That's what is available to you. You have to develop a level of pride that makes you want to perform. Sometimes you can develop that on the job, sometimes you have to develop it somewhere else. Once you have that feeling, you will be on your way. This captain had never received an *A* in his life. Once he got one, he wanted a million of them. He wanted so much to do better each day. An *A* was all he could think about. Once you develop that level of pride you don't care what anybody else thinks. You don't care whether or not they praise you. You no longer require stroking . . . you perform because it makes you feel good! It is called *PRIDE.*

A lady who worked for me several years ago, as my administrative officer, a GS-7, came by my office one day and sat down and began telling me her sad story. She had been a GS-7 forever and she was never going to get promoted again. I asked her, "What are you doing for yourself?" She said, "Well, I'm taking a night school course occasionally and in the spring of '89 I will get an Associate's Degree." I said, "Why not go for a Bachelor's Degree? The reason I make that suggestion is because so many people get their Associate's Degree and then they assume that because they received a diploma they have accomplished something and are not inclined to go back and finish the work to get a four-year degree. There are very few fields where you can get by with an Associate's Degree. If you want to go to school, get a four-year degree." She finally signed up. She went to school for a semester and came back and said, "Here's my report card to show you I went." She had received a *C*. I said, "That's pretty impressive. Everybody got a *C*. Except the people who got *A*'s and *B*'s." The next quarter she got an *A*. I told her that was very good. I knew she could do that all along, but I was waiting for her to discover it. Then I pointed out that some people get two or three of those. The next quarter she got two *A*'s.

For the last year before she moved on to another organization, she was required to come by every quarter to get a letter from me authorizing her for an academic overload. She was carrying 25 hours of undergraduate work in her spare time. She was also raising two children and working full-time. She was an honor student. She did not get an Associate's Degree in the spring of '89. However in the fall of '89, she received a Bachelor's Degree. She is a GS-11 today. She was promoted twice before she received her degree. Her promotions were not because she had a degree, but because everyone knew she was working on a degree, knew her level of performance and wanted to hire her.

That's what is available with a little bit of enthusiasm. Once people start, you don't have to pat them on the head every day. Once they get started down the road doing things better every day, they will carry on by themselves. Not only will they carry on by themselves, their enthusiasm will spread throughout your organization. I could do nothing more for this lady on the job, so I merely offered her a way to develop her pride in her own best interest. The pride and enthusiasm she gained while at school was too important to her to leave at home, so she brought it to work every day. Everyone became infected!

Your obligation as a supervisor is to provide your subordinates the opportunity and the encouragement to move forward. As a supervisor, you owe that to everybody in your organization. If you are not in charge of others, and are dissatisfied with your lot in life, do not wait for your supervisor to come along and lead you by the hand. Accept full responsibility for your future and step out smartly. Don't assume your boss cares and will help–you are probably right, but don't bank on it–you may be wrong. The choice is yours. If you are at the bottom, and you want to move out, this is the way you do it.

To give you an idea of how this applies to your job, let me tell you about my recent hardship tour. I was invited to go to the Bahamas for two days to speak to the employees of a corporation. These people had what was perceived to be a serious safety problem. Since they thought I knew something about safety, I was asked to come and speak to them. They did not have a safety problem. They had an attitude problem. A serious attitude problem. That attitude problem is what we talked about for the two days I was there. I talked to 2,200 people in the organization. A year later they sent me a copy of their corporate magazine which reported that the greatest success story of the previous year was at the Bahamas location. They had reduced the cost for workman's compensation from the projected cost by a million dollars in one year!

That is the difference you can make without expending any additional effort. It is doing things smarter and better. Those people were hurting themselves on the job every day through stupidity and there were no rules. They were very proud of being able to do their job while they were injured. I suggested they needed to try doing their jobs without being injured. They would see how simple it was. Besides that, it doesn't hurt! I explained that if they worked for me, I wouldn't allow them to work that way because I couldn't afford the million bucks. Neither could that company, but they had never done anything about it. An attitude change can do that.

Eglin AFB owns the largest vehicle fleet in the entire Air Force. Eglin personnel drove more miles than anybody in the world. When I came to Eglin in 1980 as the Chief of

Safety, we crashed and burned, on a regular basis, somewhere between 50 and 80 vehicles a year. When I saw that I was obviously shocked. I asked my chief of ground safety, "What are we doing about this?" He cited the same rule: The National Safety Council says a 3 percent reduction per year is a good goal and better than most organizations accomplish! I computed that it would take me 'til I was 180 years old to get the statistic down to where I wanted it. So we changed the rules. I said, "Let's assume that 3 percent per year is not good enough. Let's assume that the goal is zero accidents next year." Everybody thought I was insane. In 1988, in 10.5 million miles driven, we had one reportable accident. In 1989, to prove it wasn't a fluke, we drove 13.5 million miles and we had one reportable accident. We never hit zero, but if we had taken the National Safety Council's guidelines, we would still be operating at the rate of 30 or 40 accidents per year! We didn't get there by *accident*, or because we were smarter than anybody else. We got there because we said that's where we are going to go. We knew where the rate should be and we committed ourselves to achieving the goal.

Earlier I discussed the Presidential decree on the National Safety Council guidelines. It arrived saying we were to injure 118 folks. We had to decide where to start. We didn't know where we stood. So the first thing we had to do was to determine how we were doing in relation to the President's decree. Our records indicated we had averaged 64 reportable injuries for the three previous years. The presidential guidance set our goal (our pro rata share) at 118. You should know that all the weapons you saw on television during the Persian Gulf War were developed and tested at Eglin. We were in the weapons test business, where everything touched was designed to blow up. In this high risk environment, we were operating about 50 percent *BELOW* the Federal average for injuries on the job. That in itself was pretty impressive. The assumption was that because we were doing so well, we couldn't do any better. Nobody had ever tried. The goal was 118 injuries. The commander here at that time said go for the 118 injuries, down 3 percent per year. I said, "You gotta be joking! That's twice the number that we have actually injured in the past!" He said, "Don't make it too tough." That was his goal. My goal was down 3 percent per year from the 64 we had been having. After five years ended in the fall of 1988, we had reduced the 64 injuries per year by another 60 percent. At the time, Eglin, in a very high risk environment, operated at about 18 to 20 percent of the national average for civilian employees injured on the job. That is absolutely spectacular and they didn't get there by coincidence. They got there because they decided that's what they knew they could achieve. They are still working on that number every day and are still trying to push it down every day. The basic premise of continuous improvement is very simple: you are never finished because the job can always be done better. As I said before, TQM is not a program with a start and a finish. It must become a way of life!

That's the kind of spectacular performance you can achieve. If you would establish your goals and assume that nothing is impossible, assume that it is important to do it better, become a little bit enthusiastic and press on, you can do anything. When you do that, you will be amazed at the outcome. You will create a change and I guarantee you it will create a lot of stress. More stress than you have ever encountered in your whole life because nobody wants to change. If you never change, you can do your job with minimal effort, almost in your sleep, and certainly without much thinking. Most people are very comfortable with the status quo. They love it there. They have been there forever. You know what they say, "This is the way we have always done it." If anybody ever tells you that, ask them how long they have been doing it that way. If they have been doing it that way for a week, they are a week behind the rest of the world. If they have been doing it that way for a year, they are a year behind the rest of the world. If they have been doing it that way for ten years, then they are ten years behind the rest of the world. You can make no progress without change. I guarantee you, change is going to generate some stress.

STRESS

Earlier I promised information on stress. Let me tell you a short story about stress management and where stress fits in my belief. This is a two-minute stress management seminar. Four years ago I was invited to speak at a conference where the speaker just before me was a psychologist. He did a one-hour stress management seminar. I have since tried to get him to go around with me to do his stress management hour but he won't, so I have learned part of his speech and I do it for him. Basically, he spends an hour explaining and defining stress, how it works and why it works, what it does to you and how terrible it is. By the completion of his talk, he has the audience sweating blood. He has them convinced they have a strong possibility of dying of stress–today! Then he offers a solution. "For $100 per hour, you can come to my office and I'll fix you. Now I know most of you can't afford that so I am going to give you a simple home remedy for stress that you can use anytime, anyplace when things get out of hand."

He continued, "If you are under an enormous amount of stress, sit down, and close your eyes, and visualize yourself in a comfortable place where you would rather be. Let's assume we are in Colorado. You can see the mountains and a beautiful valley. The flowers are beautiful, and the birds are singing, the wind is blowing through the trees and you can hear the babbling brook. It is a spectacularly beautiful place. If I could have you wired while I describe this beautiful setting, I could prove that your heart rate has decreased, your blood pressure has decreased, your temperature has decreased and your stress is near zero. You are more relaxed. If I talked to you for five more minutes I could have you all asleep. This is the way you combat stress." He finished his speech by reminding them that this concept was free, and could be used anytime, under any circumstances.

As he sat down, I was trying to figure out how I was going to make the transition from his speech to mine, which was obviously going to generate a lot of stress. I said, "I have known this man for 17 years. He is a highly qualified psychologist so I am not going to challenge or argue with anything he has said. What I want to do is give you one more opportunity to practice this technique in a slightly different environment. I want you to visualize yourself in an airplane, going straight down at 600 miles an hour with no wings on the aircraft. Now close your eyes and wish you were somewhere else. I don't think you are going to like the outcome!"

I am not going to try and tell you that stress is good for you in any way, shape or form. However, stress is a part of every day of your life. The stress level goes up and down depending on the kinds of decisions you are making and how important they are on that particular day. When you are making the most important decisions stress is very high. When your life is at risk, stress goes off the chart. That is not the time to close your eyes and wish you were somewhere else. That is the time you open your eyes very wide, assume responsibility for your future and step up and make intelligent decisions and press on. It is vital if you want to survive in this world. Once you have learned to make good quality decisions, under that level of stress, things will really start coming together for you. If you can learn to react in that manner routinely, your stress will go down, because your confidence will go up.

You should enter into a high stress environment with a lot of enthusiasm and courage, so you don't quit before you finish. You also need a good amount of innovation so you don't do everything the hard way. Regardless of the outcome, you should be prepared to accept the responsibility for your decisions. If the results were good, remember what you did so you can repeat your performance. If the results were not so good, learn from your mistakes so you can do better next time. After you have made this your way of doing business for a short time, you will develop a level of pride that is far beyond anything you have ever known. Then you will be at that point I talked about earlier where you feel that pride deep down inside that forces you to do your best every minute of every day. You will no longer care what your boss or anyone else thinks, because you will be performing better than anyone else, possibly even better than your boss. At that point, life becomes amazingly simple.

I end this section with a small but provocative idea. No doubt, all of you have heard the famous quote of Abraham Lincoln, "Things come to those who wait." Perhaps few, if any of you, know the rest of the quote, the words that are rarely uttered, "But only the things left behind by those who hustle." Thus it is in this world, ladies and gentlemen. You can accept the challenge, escape from the box and get out and hustle. You can become a leader and assist others in their attempt to escape from the box. Or, you can join the ranks of those unfortunates, like the folks in the band marching in the parade, who are following the mounted posse. You can wait and see what is left.

The choice is yours!

PART THREE

Let Me Try

"LET ME TRY"

"The choice is up to you." That is, the choice to try. But is that always true? What about the frustration you feel when you are denied the opportunity to try? If you recall, earlier in this book I talked about the first day a theoretical expert on TQM came to Eglin Air Force Base to spread the word from on high. Near the end of his presentation he casually mentioned this one minor problem with the concept, "No one has yet figured out a way to get everyone to sign up to participate." If you remember, I volunteered to do that part for him. He promptly responded, "sit down and shut up, no one asked you." To say I was upset by his rejection would be a gross understatement. My blood was still boiling when I returned to my office an hour later. As I sat down at my desk, I grabbed a felt tipped marker and in enormous letters across my desk pad wrote, "*LET ME TRY*!!!"

For the next several weeks that desk pad began to take on new meaning. That wasn't the first time I had been told to sit down and shut up, nor would it be the last. But, each day when I walked in and saw those three words, "Let me try!!!," I thought of other incidents. Some had happened to me and others I had only witnessed or read about. With each new idea came a new cryptic note on my desk pad. Eventually, those cryptic notes were the beginnings of this section of the book you now hold in your hands.

There are various levels of frustration. I had an experience during my period of captivity in North Vietnam that led to an extraordinarily high level of frustration, even compared to the constant frustration we felt throughout the totality of that experience. In May 1968, an American POW was thrown into our cell and we were told to "take care of him." He had been beaten so badly that he had lost touch with reality. He wouldn't speak to us, and he would neither eat nor drink. It was readily apparent "taking care of him" was going to be a real challenge.

After several days of discussion among ourselves it was agreed that this man would die unless we did something drastic and soon. The next day we undertook what I consider to be the most demanding effort of my life. We decided to force feed the gentleman. We had no experience, no training, no equipment, and no idea how we would accomplish this feat. But, we did try!

It took four very determined men to physically restrain this man, force the food into his mouth, and then hold his nose in order to force him to swallow so he could breathe again. It took slightly over one hour for each meal. We went through that exercise twice each day, for almost one year. The frustration we endured during that year, knowing that without a miracle the man would die, overwhelmed me some days. But, at least we tried. Later the man was moved back into solitary confinement, and with no one to care for him, he subsequently died in captivity.

Not even counting the events just described, the summer of 1968 was, by many measures, one of the low points of my captivity experience. Just prior to the arrival of the man who would not eat, I had a minor disagreement with a guard. I ended up with a broken jaw for my trouble. Since there was no medical care available, it did not heal quickly. The only way I can describe the pain associated with my injury is to ask you to imagine an ice pick stuck in your left ear for about four months. Needless to say, eating was difficult and resulted in my losing nearly 50 pounds. I had now achieved what we laughingly called our fighting trim. For me, that was slightly less than 100 pounds. As my health deteriorated and the days got hotter, I started developing boils. During a 90-day period, I had 221 boils–from the top of my head to my feet. I should have died that summer, but I didn't have time because I lived with this other American who had a greater problem. He needed to be spoon fed to stay alive. He needed my help and the Vietnamese let me try.

When you know something must be done, but for lack of knowledge, or appropriate tools, you are unable to succeed, the frustration is quite high. However, that frustration is insignificant when compared to the frustration you feel when you know something must be done, you have more than adequate knowledge, you have more tools than you could ever hope to use, and you are denied the opportunity to try.

Do you ever wonder what would happen if we just turned people loose, with no restriction and let them try–if we allowed them to escape from the box? Think back to the very early pages of this book when I was describing the tap code and I was expounding on our church call held in prison. I discussed the tremendous value (whether we were religious or not) of honoring church call at the same time or, as I expressed it, "all rowing the boat in the same direction." I talked about how we tend to underrate and under-utilize teamwork in this country, even though it is free! Now I want to take you to a new level of understanding of this concept. What do you suppose we could accomplish as Americans if we were not only allowed to try, but were allowed to work as a team? Do you think we could gain a competitive advantage? I think so.

In the spring of 1992, I got wind of a new start-up operation, and from all accounts it was going to be a real back-breaker. It would start almost immediately, there would be very limited resources, production had to accelerate at an unimaginable rate from day one, and there would be no formal training. The headquarters was actively seeking a leader. I called and said, "Let me try." They did.

The production graph below shows a horizontal axis, which represents time in days and a vertical axis which represents production in thousands of units.

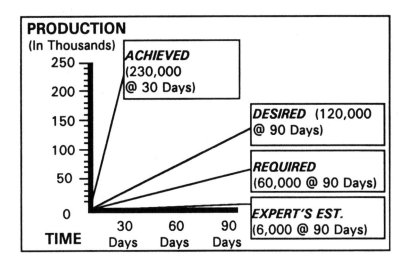

The absolute minimum level of production to stay in business was determined to be 60,000 complete units in the first 90 days. Due to the concern at the headquarters about failure rates, we were requested to attempt to achieve 120,000 units in the first 90 days. Naturally, all the industry experts were looking over our shoulders, criticizing, and predicting the standard doom and gloom. One industry analyst was even bold enough to make a prediction. He estimated that if everything went perfectly and we were lucky besides, we could produce 6,000 units in the 90 days.

As previously mentioned, operations had to start almost immediately. We had a few days to organize via telephone. We then had one meeting with about 28 people that lasted four hours. We developed a vision, a plan of attack, a couple of milestones and we went to work.

The afternoon before operations began, I received a phone call from the headquarters. They asked for my honest assessment of the feasibility of achieving success in producing 60,000 units in 90 days. I allowed as how it should not be too difficult–we planned to do it the first day! Actually, we did not hit that mark; we only produced 35,000 units the first day. But, as you can plainly see on the graph, we completed 230,000 units in the first 30 days. Why? We were allowed to try. We were allowed to work as a team. And, no one told us how to do it!

To give you a complete picture, you must have a bit more information about the production operation just described. Of the eleven key leadership positions in the organization, nine were filled by people who were doing this in their spare time. We all had other full-time jobs. All the people involved were volunteers and received no pay! None of the eleven leaders had any prior training or experience in this type of work. And, perhaps most important of all, when I selected my leaders I picked 10 people out of 400 names I had been given. I made all my selections in less than four hours and I did that over the phone. I merely reached into the pile of papers, pulled out one name and I called. I did not ask about any of the standard criteria like experience and education, any of the illegal things such as age, sex, race, or any of the things we might normally use to screen applicants. I asked one question: "Are you willing to accept full responsibility for achieving this task in your region?" The first person to say yes in each region was the designated leader.

If you want some additional icing on your cake, let me tell you about our failure rate. It is always assumed that if you are in too big of a hurry, you may only produce junk. Our reliability rate was 92 percent!

The next time you want to know just how much more could be accomplished in this great country of ours, look back at our graph. If you like those results, let your people try; let them escape from the box.

The lines on the graph struck me to be analogous with some other standards used in our country, so I labeled each line in my mind.

Like the doom predicted by the experts, the 6,000 units line represents what the Federal Government, and all the experts inside the Washington beltway, believe is available in our country. The 60,000 units line represents what I call the "American Standard, or minimum satisfactory." The

120,000 units line is where we hope to go someday, through TQM or some other magic formula. The success represented by the 230,000 units line, the line that goes nearly straight up, the line that represents what we actually accomplished, is available everyday in this country, for free!

COMMITTED LEADERSHIP

It would not be fair to move onto the next subject without explaining what we were producing. I was the original state coordinator in charge of getting Ross Perot's name on the ballot for the 1992 presidential election in Florida. We had to produce 60,312 (to be exact) signed petitions and we had 90 days to accomplish the task. As they say, the rest is history. I believe we very clearly demonstrated the enormity of the untapped human potential that exists in this country if we will only let people try. We demonstrated beyond a shadow of doubt how to develop a competitive advantage.

I am frequently reminded of a story I heard once. It was told by a gentleman named Louis Tice, one of the finest speakers I have had the privilege of hearing. He was trying to make a point about people with far more capability than they are credited with, but who aren't allowed to try. As Mr. Tice relates the story, it was the last few seconds of a critical football game and the home team trailed by only one point. They had the ball near mid-field and it was fourth down. The only possibility was one last desperate pass for a touchdown. About that time, the team's youngest place-kicker stepped up to the coach and asked to be allowed to try a field goal. The coach looked at the young man in total disbelief, but, due to the futility of the situation said, "OK."

The young kicker raced onto the field and very calmly kicked a 62-yard field goal, the longest field goal in history. In the jubilation that followed the coach kept asking, "How did you ever do that?" The young man just smiled and replied, "Coach, I have been doing that for three months in practice. You just wouldn't ever let me try in a game."

In case you wonder about the story told by Louis Tice, allow me to provide you a bit of déjà vu. In November 1992, I was returning from a speaking engagement in Berlin. When I landed at JFK airport on Saturday afternoon, I had about three hours to kill before my next flight. As I languished in the Delta Crown Room, I was watching a football game between two colleges whose names I do not even remember. With about 10 seconds left in the game, the team trailing by one point had the ball near mid-field. Their options were a desperation pass, or a 52-yard field goal.

The first-string field goal kicker had been injured and was not available, further complicating the problem. The second-string kicker had never been successful beyond 39 yards in a game. With a shrug of capitulation, the coach sent the second-string kicker on to the field. The young man's kick not only cleared the cross bar to win the game, but the ball went far into the grandstand. In an interview following the game, the kicker was asked how he could so casually perform such a feat under such incredible pressure. With equal calmness he explained that he had been kicking 72-yard field goals routinely in practice for a year. Nobody would ever let him try in a game.

Let me take you back to 1988 and the finals of the NCAA basketball tournament. Here we find similar circumstances, a difficult situation, and a coach with a slightly different perspective on the world. The University of Kansas Jayhawks entered the tourney unrated and unseeded, having had a relatively poor season. In the quarter-finals, the Jayhawks found themselves facing the number one team in the nation. At the end of the game, the kids from Kansas were the winners and their opponents were no longer number one. Two nights later in the semifinals, the Jayhawks found themselves in the unenviable position of opposing the new Number One team, and they won again. Now that group from Kansas, still unrated but becoming better known, was in the NCAA finals for the National Championship.

Perhaps no team had ever faced a more difficult challenge. The outcome certainly wasn't assured. As the five starting players from Kansas gathered in the middle of the floor, awaiting tip-off time, they were surrounded by the rest of their teammates urging them on. At that moment, University of Kansas coach, Larry Brown, stepped into the middle of the gathering for some final words. Most of you have witnessed such an event, each player straining and stretching to get one hand into this giant handshake, each player straining to create the oneness of effort required to meet the challenge ahead. Whether it was a twist of fate or merely good fortune, there was an extra hand in the pile that night and it held a live broadcast microphone that recorded what I consider one of the simplest, yet most profound comments I have ever heard.

Coach Larry Brown's last words to his men before the opening tip-off was, "Don't be afraid to win." They were not afraid to win. They did win. Though I never attended K.U., I have never been so proud of the fact that I grew up in Kansas. Larry Brown set a leadership example that night that we would all do well to emulate. He let his team know he trusted them and had great confidence in their ability. With five simple words he told them very clearly he not only was going to let them try, he would accept nothing less. It is a message every manager and supervisor in every aspect of our nation should transmit immediately to all of their charges, "Don't be afraid to win." Unfortunately, the message is not being communicated.

Instead, denying people the opportunity to do what they know how to do has virtually become a way of life in this country. It has been the recognition of that problem and the associated frustration that led me to start speaking to groups across the country. If I had the ability to make one small chink in the armor of the defenders of status quo, then I had an obligation to try. I would be less than truthful if I told you my efforts had met with roaring success. The reasons I am given for "why" we can't do certain things do more than frustrate me. They absolutely amaze me. I want to share a series of anecdotes that I hope will also amaze you. Furthermore, I hope they will cause you to look inwardly and consider how you would react under similar circumstances.

I decided to really get serious about creating major changes in organizations in the fall of 1980. I had been assigned the position of Director of Safety at Eglin Air Force Base, the largest safety office in the Air Force other than the one at Air Force Headquarters. This was not what you would call a choice assignment. No one wanted to be in safety. The opportunity for promotion was essentially zero, and everyone knew the only purpose the safety office served was to slow progress and disapprove everything. I saw this as potentially the end of my career. In the long run, it turned out to be the beginning of my career. I had as my vision from day one to change the image of *safety pukes* as we were affectionately known, from obstacles to progress, to critically important members of a winning team.

Almost as if someone were challenging my sincerity, two events occurred my first day on the job that were going to become instrumental to long term success. Less than 30 minutes after I arrived, I had a visit by a lieutenant colonel who announced that he was the leader of a team from the Air Force Leadership, Management and Development Center. His assigned task was to conduct a management survey of all the 58 units assigned to Eglin. It would involve a survey of 108 management responsibilities to determine the quality of management practices. All assigned personnel from top to bottom would complete the survey which would indicate how superiors and subordinates were viewed. I explained I had been in my job for 30 minutes and didn't even know anyone, let alone have an opinion. I was excused from the survey.

Two weeks later the survey was completed. The scores were tabulated, the final reports were written, and it was time for the colonel and his team to out brief the results to the general and his staff. I don't suppose I will ever forget that event. Near the end, a chart was put up that clearly announced that the Director of Safety organization was the poorest managed of all 58 organizations on the base! Dead last. We were each handed written copies of the final report with the results broken out by organization. We were told the results were so poor across the board that the team would return in three to four months for a follow-up survey. Then we were excused.

I returned to my office, got my three directors together, gave them each their portion of the report and told them to study it for 24 hours. The next day we would meet to discuss what to do. You must remember, I had only been there for two weeks and I barely knew my directors. Worse than that, I still had not identified all their personality quirks. It did not take long at the meeting the next morning to find out why we had been judged poorest managed. The first director hadn't found time to read the report yet. The second director had read it but wanted more time to study it. The third director had thrown it in the trash and loudly pronounced it to be "worthless bullshit." Then, to add to the confusion, the second and third directors, who were competing contemporaries, engaged in open hostilities about which one of them should be blamed for the apparent failure.

COURAGE, AGAIN

After breaking up the argument, and putting forth some very clear guidance on the behavior required of senior managers (notice I don't refer to them as leaders yet), I returned to my office to contemplate my problems. It was during my contemplation that I received one of those "once in a lifetime" pleasant surprises.

A young man from my organization, with no supervisory responsibilities, walked into my office and asked if he could have a few minutes. I had only met him once or twice in my brief tour, but did recognize him as a member of the group under the third director. In his hand this young man was holding the final report his director had deposited in the trash. He told me he had not had enough time to study it completely, but he had glanced over it and felt he could provide me with perspective on some of the problem areas and possibly some suggestions. All he needed was my permission to proceed, which he got in about one-tenth of a second!

Between this young man and one other even younger man, I got the lowdown on all the infighting and power brokering in the organization. I also received a wealth of knowledge about virtually every individual's strengths, weaknesses, and frustrations. As a total organization, we then held a meeting. It was a meeting where all cards were played face up and everyone was allowed to speak their mind, respectfully. Later, I named the meetings "Adult Conversations" and it is a practice I teach to corporations where I consult. We all left the meeting with a far better understanding of our problems and their solutions. More importantly, every one left the meeting with a new vision of the organization, where we were going, and how we would get there. There was a new attitude, one that would become a way of life in the Safety Office.

As advertised, the management survey team returned about three months later. And as before, following the survey there was a formal out-briefing. However, the content of the briefing had changed dramatically. The Director of Safety organization had shown a statistically significant improvement in 104 of the 108 areas surveyed (96 percent). In 90 days, the organization transitioned from the poorest managed on the base to the best managed. We never looked back!

The total credit for that miraculous occurrence belongs to one young man who wanted to make a difference, who felt he had the ability to do so, who had the courage to ask, and who fortunately worked for a man who let him try.

Building on that success was relatively easy and was partly due to the subtle message I had sent to all the people in the organization without ever realizing the significance at the time. This involved the second event, which I mentioned occurred on my first day on the job.

At about 10:00 a.m. I received my first phone call in my new position. It was from an old friend who held a key position in the weapons test organization. He started friendly, but I could tell by the tone of his voice this was not just a casual call to welcome me on board. He explained they had a very high-priority test they wanted to proceed with, but were unable to because they could not get my safety organization to approve the test plan. I promised to check into it and get right back to him. I called the office in charge of such things and asked the project officer, a major, to come see me.

Upon his arrival I asked the major about the status of the project and he reported they had sent him the test plan and he had disapproved the plan. I said, "Then what did you do?" His answer should not have surprised me, but it did. He said, "Nothing, I am waiting for them to send me a new plan." When I asked if he told them why it was disapproved, or offered any suggestions for how the plan could be changed, he merely pointed out to me that wasn't his job. Their job was to develop test plans and his job was to approve or disapprove those plans.

Since I had only been in the job for two and a half hours and had never even met the major prior to that moment, it seemed rather inappropriate to bite the major's head off. I must admit, however, that was certainly my first inclination. His answer had just confirmed my life-long beliefs about too many safety professionals. At the same time, it reinforced my determination to show them another way to do business.

As calmly as I could, I told the major, "Your job just changed. Effective immediately you will assume that people smarter than you and me decided these tests are required. Our job is to accomplish the Air Force mission at the earliest possible time, at the least possible cost, and insure no one gets injured en route. And from this day forward, you will do everything in your power, including planning tests, to guarantee that we (safety) are a part of the solution and not a part of the problem. We will become a critical part of the Air Force team. Furthermore, on the way back to your office, I want you to stop in every room and explain my concept to everyone in this building." Earlier I stated I had sent a subtle message to my people. Well, looking back, maybe it wasn't so subtle, but it was clear. I have always believed that one of my strengths is that I am rarely misunderstood!

After I had been taking a similar message to Air Force audiences and civic groups around the country for a couple of years, I started receiving an occasional request from corporations. Eventually, I went through the bureaucratic red tape and obtained permission from the Air Force to moonlight. You can't just go out and find a part-time job when you are in the military. You must have written permission from your boss. Once that permission was obtained I formed my own corporation and got serious.

I had only been speaking professionally for about five months when I received my introduction to Total Quality Management. As you will recall from my earlier discussion, the very first thing that struck me about TQM was how close the concept paralleled the basic theme of my own presentation. It was at that time I started applying my concepts more specifically to quality improvement efforts. However, I was very careful to point out that "I do not teach TQM, I only talk about similar concepts called leadership and common sense." My concept has basically the same aims as TQM, but I don't attempt to teach something someone else invented.

Among my early clients was a production operation in the northeastern part of our country. (I mentioned this corporation in the section on "responsibility.") I had been invited to speak to approximately 800 members of their management club. Following my presentation, the corporate president told me he would like all 12,000 of his employees to hear my message and he introduced me to his vice president for human resources who would be in charge of making the arrangements. A brief discussion led us to believe it would be best if I came in soon and spent one day just getting acquainted with their organization and developing a plan.

Two weeks later, I spent one very full day at their facility. As I toured the various shops in the plant, I asked lots of questions and the answers I received puzzled me a great deal. On the surface, it appeared to be a very modern, smooth running operation. On the other hand, the attitudes of many of the people, including some supervisors, did not mesh with the outward appearance. The answers to some questions helped clear the picture. First, I was told that the mother corporation had been demanding 10 percent profitability from this specific plant for over two years, yet they were operating just barely over 7 percent. Additionally, first-time quality (the number of produced items that work the first time they are used, without being repaired) at this plant was only 41 percent. To further compound their problems, over 75 percent of their products came off the production line in the last week of every month. I have never been involved in manufacturing in my life, but even I could see why they were in trouble.

Late in the afternoon I met with the vice president for human resources and another gentleman who was a full time organizational structures consultant for them. I expressed a strong interest in trying to help them achieve some dramatic improvements and told them that during my discussions out in the plant the idea had received favorable comments. At that point the human resource V.P. said, "It is possible you could do some good here because this is a high-tech operation and these are all highly educated people. However, I'm not so sure you could get results at our other plant down south. It is a low-tech operation and I'm not certain they would follow your train of thought."

I asked what the problems were at the other plant and was told that basically they had one large problem. They had not met their production schedule for two years. They were paying exorbitant penalties to the customer.

At the risk of sounding like a smart aleck, I offered them a proposal. I offered to come to work for their corporation full-time for 30 days. I would split my time between the two plants as appropriate. During that 30-day period I would double their first-time quality at the high-tech plant and simultaneously double production at the low-tech plant. At the same time, we could be doing a comparison of which group responded most favorably to my message. If I succeeded at both plants, my fee would be $100,000 plus expenses. If I failed to meet the goal at either one or both plants, my efforts would be free! I then explained how I would proceed at each plant using my concept of "Adult Conversations."

When employees participate in my "Adult Conversations" exercise, they are allowed to identify any problem at any level within the organization or its operation. Furthermore, they are "allowed" to provide potential solutions. If they are unable or unwilling to proceed to the solution step, the exercise becomes meaningless and it will be terminated. Assuming the exercise continues, they can be assured that if their suggestion is put into action, they will be responsible for guaranteeing its success. Then, and only then, will they discover the complexities of responsibility.

Following my overview of the "Adult Conversations" exercise, I asked for questions. The first question came from the organizational structures consultant. He said, "Are you what is known as a charismatic leader?" I told him I had never been called that, nor did I claim to be such. Then he asked, "Then why do you think you can do these things where we have failed?" I replied, "That is quite simple. There is a significant difference between me and you. You do not believe these things can be achieved, therefore you will never try. I know they can, so I will try." They thanked me for my time, said they would think about it and call me in a few days. That meeting took place over two years ago and I never heard from them again.

The last statement I made as I left their office was, "Let me try."

Epilogue

I tried to sell the picture I painted in 1984 which I mentioned at the beginning of this book, but nobody wanted to buy it. Next, I tried to give it away and I couldn't even pull that off. They then built the conference center at Eglin and they were looking for a piece of art for the lobby and I offered my painting. They said they didn't need it. Eventually I put it in my own office and it hung there for about a year.

Shortly thereafter, they built the museum outside the west gate of Eglin with an art gallery but they didn't have any pictures in it. I saw a target of opportunity and I asked them if they wanted my picture. They said O.K. It hung in the art gallery for about three months and I had a man call me to say he had seen my picture and thought it was pretty neat. He wanted a print of it. I said, "I'm very sorry, I don't have a clue how to do that." He said, "Give me a print and I'll give you $100 for it." I said, "Don't go away!" I catch on pretty fast! It took me a year to figure out how you do that.

Eventually, I found a man in Dayton, Ohio who could do that for me. He told me I needed to decide how many I wanted, and that I should have a signed, limited edition. Eventually, we decided that 2,420 was the right number. One for each day of my captivity. Print number one represented the day I was shot down. That copy I sent to Mr. Nielsen who invented the Eagle. Print number 2,420 represents the day I gained my freedom. If you come to visit me, you will find that one hanging in my office.

Remember, there are no bad days. Some just aren't quite as good as others!

If you, your corporation, or your professional association have an interest in my services, I can be contacted at:

Positive Vectors
423 Pelham Road
Fort Walton Beach, Fl. 32547
Tel: (850) 862-5273
Fax: (850) 864-0990
email: ehubbard@gnt.net
www.edhubbardpow.com